Bankers in
the Selling Role

Bankers in the Selling Role

A CONSULTATIVE GUIDE TO CROSS SELLING
FINANCIAL SERVICES

LINDA RICHARDSON

A Wiley-Interscience Publication
JOHN WILEY & SONS
New York • Chichester • Brisbane • Toronto • Singapore

Library of Congress Cataloging in Publication Data:

Richardson, Linda,
    Bankers in the selling role.

    "A Wiley-Interscience publication."
    Includes index.
    1. Bank marketing.   I. Title.

HG1616.M3R53   332.1'068'8   80-28804
ISBN 0-471-09010-7

To
my mother and father
with gratitude and love

Preface

The concepts in this book have been drawn directly from the experience of several thousand bankers ranging from senior management and bank officers to management trainees. Observations from the field, as well as from sales seminars, provided evidence that contradicted the old adage that "salespeople are born not made."

By utilizing the consultative selling process, bankers who did not think that they had a predilection for selling developed confidence and achieved success in their new selling roles. They used their product knowledge and selling skills to individualize their sales calls, meet the needs of their customers, and generate positive sales action. In short, they *sold*, and at the same time developed long-term relationships that were mutually beneficial to the customer and the bank. Bankers generally viewed as effective salespeople also found that the consultative approach offered them additional control and flexibility, and accelerated development and refinement of their selling skills.

The objective of this book is to create an awareness and acceptance of the role of sales in banking and to help bankers plan and conduct effective sales interviews.

The consultative approach to sales in banking presented in this book is designed to assist bankers in their roles as financial consultants to their customers, and, to provide them with an approach to sales that is suitable for the relationship that exists between bankers and customers. It provides bankers with an alternative to "hard" or "door to door" type selling.

One of the most common concerns voiced by bankers about selling is their desire to avoid anything that resembles hard selling. Although they reject the idea of hard selling, many untrained bankers who are placed in selling situations often resort to hard sell tactics simply because they think that is what selling is all about. Hard selling is *product* selling rather than *need* selling. Hard selling is "hard" in its approach *and* in its wear and tear on customers and bankers alike. During a hard sell, customers are often looking for a way out and bankers are searching for a way in; often bankers recite their laundry lists of products searching for a spark of interest from the customer. The antithesis of hard selling is consultative selling. By identifying customers needs and understanding the customer's situation *before* selling a product, bankers are better able to avoid the hard-sell trap. By understanding their products from their customer's point of view, they are better able to relate the products to their customer's needs. Customers buy benefits not features; they buy solutions not products. Consultative selling helps bankers understand customer needs and utilize the features and benefits of their products to respond to those needs.

Consultative banking recognizes that product knowledge is the cornerstone of selling. The consultative approach to selling helps bankers understand and communicate the product advantages that respond to customer's situation. It is the banker's ability to discuss a product relative to the customer's needs that differentiates products that are basically competitive.

The competitive advantage of a product is not so much in the operations or features of a basically competitive product but rather in the bankers' understanding of the product, how it compares to that of the competition, and their skill in communicating the value of the product to the customer's needs. If a product is basically competitive, bankers can gain a disproportionate share of the market by using the consultative sales approach. By communicating sales-oriented product information in a consultative manner, bankers can create their own marketing edge over their competitors. Among bank products, there appear to be striking similarities. Upon closer examination, bank products differ significantly in features and benefits, qualifying criteria, operational and implementation procedures, personal service, and in the overall internal design of many products. For example, for a product as common as Lock Box one bank may have fifteen pick-ups daily as compared to five by another bank. An increase in the number of pick-ups generally ensures quicker processing. One bank may have a minimum of 1000 items for a customer to qualify as a prospect for Lock Box, and another bank may require only 250 items. One bank may have an automated system and another a manual system. There are no perfect products, and there are very few, if any, identical products among banks.

Bankers can differentiate their products from those of others by being able to understand their products and discuss them from the customer's point of view. Customers are continuously evaluating products, asking "what's in it for me?" Consultative banking helps them answer that question. Consultative banking also benefits bankers since it provides them with a way to develop long-term loyal relationships that are mutually beneficial to the customer and the bank.

Consultative banking is designed to support bankers in their sales efforts by providing them with a selling framework and a process to use in marketing their credit, noncredit, and credit-related products or services.

Although the concepts in this book have been shaped by the sales experience of more than one thousand bankers, the pages of the book cannot replace individual experience. The consultative sales approach is aimed at accelerating the mastery that comes with experience. The goal of the book is to increase bankers willingness to initiate sales by developing the information, skills, and attitudes they need to be confident in their selling roles. Being effective in sales does not have to be learned the hard way by trial and error. By understanding the sales process and having a flexible framework for controlling the sales interview bankers can accelerate their effectiveness and enjoy selling.

Linda Richardson

Philadelphia, Pennsylvania
February 1981

Acknowledgments

I am grateful to all of the professionals with whom I have worked, who have shared their knowledge and experience with me. There is a special appreciation to my friend and colleague Dannie O'Connor for her support and encouragement, and to my teachers Juanita Kidd Stout, Albert Ellis, and Marc Bassin for their patience and guidance, and to Charlie McCabe at Manufacturers Hanover Trust for his vision of the role of sales in banking and his support of my initial efforts. I am also indebted to the thousands of bankers and their banks for their invaluable contributions without which this book would be incomplete.

L. R.

Contents

1
An Introduction to Consultative Banking

SALES IN BANKING

Consultative banking recognizes the importance of the role of sales in banking. Bankers are required to initiate business, to cross-sell, and to function as consultants to their customers if they expect to achieve a fair or disproportionate share of the market.

Consultative banking is an approach to sales which provides bankers with the skills required to profitably increase market share and develop long term relationships in a highly competitive environment. It provides bankers with an approach for understanding the bank's non-credit as well as credit products, a process for identifying customer needs and leading effective sales interviews and a planning and follow-up system. Consultative banking focuses on the sales communication process between bankers and customers and helps bankers look at their products and services from the customer's point of view. It appreciates the value that the customer derives from the sale. It is the antithesis of door to door selling since the needs of the customers are the focal point of the sale. Bankers who use the consultative approach can recognize and maximize opportunities by discussing alternatives with customers and assisting them in making decisions with confidence.

Consultative banking is a process for planning, implementing, and nurturing a relationship. It provides bankers with tools they need to link their bank's capabilities with their customer's situation and increase their ability to uncover needs, solve problems or improve situations.

Consultative banking aims at building long term relations which are beneficial to the customer and to the bank. Bankers must conclude sales which are not only in the best interest of the bank, protecting the bank's profit margin, but also in the best interest of the customer. Relationships which are mutually beneficial should be the rule, not the exception. In the competitive environment of banking, it behooves bankers to equitably meet and satisfy customer needs as they satisfy the requirements of the bank. Mutually beneficial agreements are achievable when needs and alternatives are understood.

The following case history illustrates a mutually beneficial sale.

Background. A company that was a customer of the bank had a check-processing system with numerous problems, such as incorrect serial numbers, lost checks, and late processing.

Bank intervention. A banker became aware of the company's problem during a follow-up call and arranged a meeting with the product specialist from the Cash Management Unit to discuss the problem. During the joint call, the product specialist introduced the idea of a special indexing process in which the customer could save time, reduce costs, and reduce problems. The customer agreed to try the new system.

Analysis. The banker's objective for the follow-up call was to discuss the customer's needs. The banker was able to apply his product knowledge when a problem surfaced. By calling in the product manager or specialists to discuss an alternative, not only were the customer's problems solved but the bank's internal marketing objective of converting customers from regular sorting to special indexing was also achieved. Both the customer and the bank were able to reduce costs and save time. By satisfying a customer's needs and correcting a problem, the banker nurtured and strengthened a valued relationship. The bank was able to increase the cost by three cents per item (over 30%). The customer was so satisfied with the efficiency of the new system that he converted one other company account and sought Cash Management Consultation for his headquarters.

In this example, the banker applied his product knowledge to a customer's need. By striving for a mutually beneficial arrangement, he satisfied the need and succeeded in cross-selling a product enhancement. (The term "cross-selling" means providing additional bank products or services to current customers.) The banker discussed the product from the customer's perspective, pointing out the benefits that would accrue to the customer with the new system. At the same time, the banker guarded and promoted the bank's interests.

RESISTANCE TO SELLING

Although the consultative approach to sales in banking affords bankers the opportunity to serve as advisors and consultants to their customers, not all bankers are comfortable with the idea of selling. Selling appears to many bankers as a departure from the profession they originally selected. Previously bankers had, at best, passive selling roles in which they waited for business to walk in the door. Because of the highly competitive environment, management in banks throughout the country have redefined bankers' roles and include in their primary responsibilities active sales solicitation. The change from passive to active selling has been stimulated by aggressive marketing from within the banking industry, competition from nonbanking institutions, inroads of foreign banks, technology, regulations, sophisticated cash management from corporations, and the changing loan environment. The keen competitive environment has caused the senior management of both regional and money center banks to emphasize the sale of noncredit and credit-related products in their marketing plans as a way to develop, expand, and protect their market share. Bankers who chose banking as a "nonselling" profession are now caught in the transition to an aggressive and still-changing banking industry.

Many bankers, both new and experienced, find themselves having to reconcile the apparent contradiction that has surfaced in their profession. Many bankers who resist selling basically do so because they think that all selling is high pressure. As long as they associate sales with high-pressure tactics and misrepresentations, they will rightly reject it as unprofessional and unworthy of banking.

Fortunately, not all selling is high pressure or disreputable. Consultative selling is the antithesis of high-pressure sales. Perhaps by differentiating the various kinds of selling, it may be possible to isolate the negative image and contrast it with the positive benefits that can accrue to customers and bankers alike through consultative sales.

IMAGE OF SELLING

A look at the image of selling over the past century may shed some light on the negative response sometimes associated with sales. From the beginning, the image of sales was in serious trouble. The "snake oil" salesman dominated selling in the 1800s. He was a charismatic individual, and as an entertainer or "healer" he charmed a naive and gullible public with his dramatizations. His monologue was filled with exaggerated claims. He was the quintessential con artist or flimflam man, traveling from town to town soliciting new victims. His objective was a quick, one-time sale. He had little or no concern for the customers' financial welfare or needs. He was a one-man show; he was the focus of the sale. By the 1870s, his shady reputation had spread throughout the country, and this stereotype still remains.

In the early part of the 1900s, the approach to selling evolved from the individual entrepreneur to salesmen who were employed by companies. Still the image of the salesman did not improve very much. Companies found it necessary to develop sales forces. Since the individuals hired by the companies had varying degrees of competence in sales, companies standardized the approach to selling. The entrepreneurial "snake oil" personality usually was not well suited to an employee status; therefore, as a way to ensure consistency in the quality and results of the presentations, a "canned" approach or "door to door" approach to selling was developed. Rather than relying on their individual inventiveness, salesmen were often programmed to make a standardized sales pitch to any and all customers regardless of their situations or needs. The pitch was high pressured, and was geared at forcing a fast and often imprudent decision to buy. The *product* became the focus of the sale. The salesman basically memorized his "script" and made the same monologue presentation to his customers. Too often he misrepresented his products and continuously found it necessary to seek a new customer base because of attrition. His legacy to the image of selling was that of the high-pressure and unethical salesman who would misrepresent the product, thén "take the money and run."

The carryover of the snake-oil and door-to-door salesman are reflected in sales today in phrases such as "drum up business" and "foot in the door." Although not all solicitation salesmen of the 1800s and early 1900s were unscrupulous or high-pressure, the overriding image of the flimflam man has prevailed in the minds of many bankers.

SALES ROLE OF BANKERS

With such a shady background behind it, it is understandable that some bankers react negatively to selling as a primary part of their jobs. Bankers who resent and resist their sales role view sales from its worst perspective, that of selling people what they do not want, really cannot use, and cannot afford, rather than examining the ways in which selling can be mutually beneficial to the customer and the seller. Numerous bank studies clearly show that customers expect bankers to consult with them on the financial alternatives available to them, to improve their situations, and to satisfy their needs. The emphasis on cash management products, both domestic and international, is an example of the kind of sophisticated service customers demand from bankers. The kind of selling that is demanded in banking is not the selling of the 1800s or the early 1900s. Today's bankers are required to be consultants, advisers, and advocates of their customers and salespeople for their banks if they are to be successful in this competitive and demanding environment. The role of consultative banking salespeople is radically different from their selling predecessors. The objective of consultative selling is the development of long-term mutually beneficial relationships, not one-time sales. Consultative selling is selling without misrepresentation or high pressure. Consultative selling is distinguished from other types of selling in its focus on the *customer's needs* rather than on the salesperson or the product. It is distinguished from high-pressure and door-to-door selling in the development of a sales dialogue rather than a monologue, and in the follow-up and nurturing that each account is given. There can be no "take the money and run" among bankers, since bankers must be concerned about the customer's financial well-being, and the last thing they want is for customers to overextend themselves. The objective of the consultative sale is to conclude deals that are mutually beneficial and mutually profitable, so that long-term relationships can be developed.

Bankers who have resisted selling should work toward redefining what selling means to them. If the quintessential salesperson in their view is a flimflam man, they are missing the consultative aspect of sales in which the customer's needs and the bank's resources to satisfy those needs complement one another. If selling connotes to bankers manipulating someone to buy what he or she doesn't want or need, they understandably should want no part of it. On the contrary, consultative sales aims at providing customers with what they need and indeed are demanding from banks or banking alternatives.

By selling or cross-selling, bankers are carving out a piece of the market while at the same time improving the customer's situation. By communicating effectively, bankers assist customers in making decisions with well-deserved confidence. Sales in banking is ethical, professional, and necessary for the customer and the bank. Sales in banking is impossible unless bankers appreciate the value of selling to customers, the bank, and the banker. Sales results of course show on the bottom line, but it is not a one-day tally that is the objective of sales in banking but rather the long-term relationship.

Although there are many effective approaches to sales, consultative selling provides bankers with a framework that can be consistently effective with a wide range of customers. It recognizes the special demands inherent in the banking industry: the wide range of credit and noncredit services, the wide range of customers and industries, and the highly competitive environment. It offers a flexible, fluid system of selling that can be applied by individual bankers to understand, control, and maximize their selling opportunities. Rather than develop a monologue presentation and monopolize the discussion, consultative bankers engage in a dialogue. They encourage customer input and guide that input through open-ended questions. Consultative bankers relate product information to the *needs* of the customers by utilizing *probing questions,* linking *features* and *benefits, fielding objections,* and *closing incrementally.* By focusing on customer needs, consultative bankers are better able to satisfy those needs and hence sell their products.

Today's customers are sophisticated, and competitors in the banking industry are aggressive. Bankers who apply consultative strategies, in a marketplace in which product knowledge, communication skills, and follow-up skills are at best inconsistently practiced, have an edge over their competitors.

Consultative banking is an effective approach to sales in banking for the 1980s. It prepares bankers to satisfy the needs of their customers while safeguarding the profit margin and market share of the bank. Consultative banking utilizes product knowledge and a sales framework that can be applied in all selling situations.

To consult effectively with their customers bankers must have:

Up-to-date sales-oriented product knowledge.

Understanding of customer needs.

Consultative selling skills.

Strategies for developing and managing accounts.

Ongoing training and reinforcement.

If any of these sales tools are missing, opportunities for sales effectiveness are significantly reduced. Bankers who have these resources have the opportunity to succeed and secure their fair share or even a disproportionate share of the marketplace.

2
Product Knowledge

PRODUCT KNOWLEDGE AS THE FOUNDATION OF SELLING

In order to maximize sales opportunities, bankers must have knowledge of a wide range of noncredit, credit-related, and credit products or services that their bank offers. Customer loyalty is not what it was, and noncredit and credit related products can be used to expand, solidify, enhance, and safeguard banking relationships. These services provide a way to open doors with prospects whose present bankers are not as aggressive, prepared, or sensitive as they might wish, and to close doors on competitors by establishing a total and satisfying banking relationship.

During the sales interview, bankers should mentally scan for selling or cross-selling opportunities. In their sales role, unless they have had a specific referral or inquiry from a customer or prospect, bankers cannot effectively approach a selling opportunity with only one product in mind. Particularly on prospect calls, bankers should probe for needs *before* initiating a discussion of a specific product. Bankers who go in prepared to discuss only one preselected product may find the interview terminated all too quickly because they do not strike a responsive chord. Bankers require an understanding of a *range of products* so that they can tap the appropriate product from their reservoir of product information, as they recognize and maximize opportunities. Doing homework prior to making a call is a first step in identifying customer needs. For example, in reading a balance sheet or a company's annual reports, bankers may identify opportunities for investment instruments such as Certificates of Deposits, Master Notes, Commercial Paper, and so on. Or in learning that the professional staff of a company travels heavily, bankers can determine that there may be an opportunity for marketing Direct Deposit of Payroll. After making assumptions concerning customer needs, bankers must be prepared with need-evoking probing questions in order to test or confirm the assumptions, to ensure that their product discussions are relevant to the customer's needs and interest.

Unless they have a general knowledge of the products important in their market area, bankers will be unable to recognize and respond to opportunities directly or indirectly signaled by customers. Without a knowledge of the bank's range of products and capabilities, bankers will not be in a position to switch gears when new needs are revealed, or to maximize opportunities that exist.

Understanding the range of products offered by their bank is often a difficult and time-consuming task for bankers. Banks throughout the country offer from 20 to 200 products to their corporate, international, retail, and personal trust customers. Bankers are not required to understand all of the products marketed by the bank, but they must be familiar with the 10 or 20 credit and non-credit products that are relevant to their specific market area. Market studies indicate that bankers are expected to know their bank's credit and noncredit capabilities (cash management, money market, and international) if they are to secure loan business and be of value to their customers. Bankers are being asked to *initiate* business and to cross-sell, since the strength of the banking relationship is dependent on the total account relationship.

What are the alternatives to providing bankers with a wide range of useful, up-to-date product knowledge information? Unfortunately, without adequate product information the alternatives are *lost opportunities* and *lost market share.* Without product information bankers are often reluctant to initiate cross-selling calls, and those who do take the initiative find it difficult to capitalize on opportunities and are reticent to try again.

Interviews with more than one thousand bankers reveal the extreme need for product knowledge. Thus it may be helpful to examine the kind of product knowledge that bankers should have during prospecting, selling, and cross-selling sales calls, and to consider a bank-wide system that could provide bankers with up-to-date sales-oriented product information on an ongoing basis.

SALES-ORIENTED PRODUCT KNOWLEDGE

Product knowledge is the foundation of sales. There are different kinds of product knowledge: technical, developmental, theoretical, generic, promotional, and sales-oriented. Although all kinds of product information are valuable, not all are appropriate for bankers with cross-selling responsibilities. Sales-oriented product information is best suited for assisting bankers in recognizing and capitalizing on sales opportunities. Too often bankers are given technical or promotional product information. Since bankers are often responsible for cross-selling as many as 10 or 20 or more products marketed in their area, it is inappropriate and impossible to give them the degree or kind of technical information that product specialists have. Likewise, the kind of product information contained in a brochure designed for the customer is not suitable, since it merely puts the banker on an equal footing with the customer and usually does not provide sufficient information for *initiating* a sale or *recognizing* a cross-selling opportunity. Bankers should have more information about products than their customers have. Bankers who call on customers need up-to-date sales-oriented product information most, and they are often the last to receive it.

RESOURCES FOR PRODUCT KNOWLEDGE

It may be helpful to examine how bankers develop their product knowledge and what resources are available to them. Bankers have individual access to product specialists; they can attend seminars or product workshops; they can discuss products with their managers; they go on "tandem" or "joint" calls with more experienced officers or specialists. They can gain product knowledge from banking literature or from banking associations, from advertisements by their bank or competitive banks. They can be coached by their managers and learn from their customers. Of course they also learn a great deal through their own experiences. All of these resources are valuable, but they are time consuming and not always readily available. An additional resource for bankers is the traditional service catalogue. Although bankers have immediate access to the information in service catalogues, the information and the catalogues themselves are usually fraught with problems.

Problems with Traditional Service Catalogues

The most obvious problems are size and accuracy. Because they are frequently cumbersome and inconvenient to carry or use, they are relegated to a shelf. And because they are so time consuming to compile, they frequently are out of date before distribution and tend to remain that way.

Equally important as the size and accuracy problems is the *kind* of information presented in the service catalogue. Too often such catalogues are technical manuals that provide little or no information relevant to a selling situation. The two or three pages dedicated to each product tend to be "get acquainted pieces" rather than viable sales tools.

Another problem with service catalogues or most product knowledge resources is that they are often treated in an isolated manner rather than as a system that is tied to an overall marketing plan and implemented as a part of training.

For these reasons the traditional service catalogue does not meet the crying need from bankers for the kind of product knowledge that is necessary during a sales call. The traditional service catalogue, although at one time a satisfactory resource, does not provide today's bankers with the kind of product information required to successfully carry out the *new responsibilities* of initiating business or selling noncredit and credit-related products that are a part of the competitive and aggressive banking industry.

Bankers should be provided with an alternative to the service catalogues to supplement the development of their product knowledge. They should request that the area responsible (marketing, a specific division, product management, training, personnel) provide up-to-date sales-oriented product information on the key products marketed by the bank. Bankers, because of time factors, should not have to develop their own product knowledge resources. The persons responsible for disseminating product information should work with those in the bank who have the most experience and expertise with the products from an operational and sales point of view. Product information should be conveniently available to all bankers with sales responsibilities, since product knowledge provides the basis of selling.

An Alternative to the Service Catalogue

As an alternative to the service catalogue, banks can individually profile each product. Rather than place all of the bank's products in one large catalogue or several divisional catalogues, the profiling approach breaks the product knowledge down into smaller, more manageable units, with one product per unit. An individual profile on each product is a viable alternative for developing and disseminating product information, since the profiles immediately solve the size problems by offering a *convenient* lightweight alternative. The individual folders also solve the content problem because they have the room and perspective to provide more than internal technical details of the products. The content of each profile should provide bankers with what they need to initiate sales calls and conduct effective sales interviews.

Each profile should be product specific. For example, in the cash management area, there could be a possibility of 5 to 10 individual profiles, such as:

Account Reconcilement.

Automated Balance Reporting.

Depository Transfer Checks.

Direct Deposit of Payroll.

Lock Box.

Zero Balance Accounts.

Other cash management products.

Each product for which there is a market focus should be profiled. A bank can have as few as 10 profiles or as many as 200. Many money centers and regional banks settle on between 30 to 50 key products to be profiled. (See pages 30 to 3 4 for lists of bank products.)

The objective of each profile is to assist bankers in recognizing and maximizing cross-selling opportunities. The profiles should be indexed and cross-referenced by industry and product group to facilitate cross selling. Of course the content of the profile is critical. It should be more comprehensive than the material usually contained in a service catalogue. Too little information is ineffectual; and too much information defeats its own purpose. Bankers require a *basic body* of information on every product for which they have cross-selling responsibilities, and this basic information should be readily available to them. The following 20 critical categories should be available to bankers for all products for which they have marketing responsibilities.

Bankers do *not* have to be *experts* in a product to initiate sales or to make appropriate cross-selling referrals, but they do need the kind of information that is apt to be required in an interview.

TWENTY CRITICAL PRODUCT KNOWLEDGE CATEGORIES
FOR A SALES INTERVIEW

Seminars, interviews, and field experience with more than one thousand bankers from regional and money center banks have identified the kinds of specific product information that are likely to be needed during sales calls.

The following categories represent the 20 aspects of a product that bankers generally need to know:

Fundamental description of the product.

Features linked with benefits.

Qualifying criteria and target market.

Customer needs.

Customer contact.

Representative customers.

Probing questions.

Objection and responses.

Competitive standing.

Case history.

Action step.

Product Implementation

Product Operations

Pricing.

In-bank contact for further information.

Start-up time.

Agreements and contracts.

Cross-sell alert.

Product family.

Exhibits.

Feedback summary.

Without a knowledge of features and benefits, bankers cannot understand a product nor can they discuss the product relative to customer needs. Unless bankers have a clear idea of who qualifies for the product, they may miss numerous opportunities. So too without probing questions bankers cannot initiate discussions, identify needs, and involve the customer. Unless bankers can respond satisfactorily to objections, they will risk losing opportunities to complete the sale or make a referral to the specialists.

Bankers require information pertaining to the 20 categories on a range of products if they are to be sensitive and responsive to customer signals and sales opportunities. Customers continually reveal needs and problems, but unless bankers understand the capabilities of the bank, they will fail to recognize opportunities, seize them, and secure a fair share of the marketplace. Following is a review of what information should be contained in each of the 20 categories.

Description

Each profile should begin with an overview of the product to provide a general understanding. The description should not be highly technical, but it should convey the *fundamental* purpose of the product. It should explain what the product is, what it does, basically how it works, and how it could possibly benefit a customer. Bankers should also be sensitive to level of sophistication of the customer in describing the product, to avoid being too elementary or too complex.

Features and Benefits

Features are the *qualities* or characteristics that the bank puts into the product; benefits are the *values* derived by the customer. Features and benefits are the heart of sales-oriented product knowledge. There is no better way to understand a product than by understanding its features and benefits, and there is no better way to sell a product than by linking the features and benefits. Features and benefits help bankers link the product with the customer's needs. They help bankers understand the product from the *customer's point of view*. Understanding and linking features and benefits enables bankers to look at a product from a sales perspective rather than from the technical or operational viewpoint. (See pages 63–65 for a discussion of features and benefits.)

Qualifying Criteria

An important factor in prospecting is recognizing the qualifying criteria for the product. Qualifying criteria means the characteristics that make a customer eligible for a product. Without knowing the qualifying criteria for products, bankers may miss sales opportunities or waste time discussing products that are not appropriate for a customer.

To determine if a customer qualifies for a product, bankers should have the following product information:

1   General criteria (target market).

2 Specific criteria that renders the customer eligible:

Volume.

Dollar.

Legal or geographic limitations.

Relationship with the bank.

Target market.

Industry focus.

For example, one of the *general criteria* for Import Letter of Credit is that the customer be an "importer of raw materials, equipment, or finished goods that qualifies for a line of credit or specific approval supported by cash." *Specific criteria* for a particular bank would include "an average letter of credit of not less than *$7,000 per issuance* and *minimum of monthly usage* of the Letter of Credit," as well as "an account with the bank."

It is very important that bankers understand the basis for any particular qualifying criterion. Although many bank's products are flexible and can be tailored to meet customer requirements, bankers should not exceed options provided by the bank unless the special requirements are warranted and approved. Customers frequently will ask for all kinds of special treatment or "bells and whistles." Bankers should find out what the customer hopes to achieve by these special requests. By applying their product knowledge, bankers can often demonstrate for the customer how a particular system that the bank uses will satisfy the stated desire. For example, when cross-selling Lock Box, bankers are often confronted by customers who prefer to keep their own lock box numbers instead of the new ones provided by the bank. On the surface, this seems very sensible. "Why can't you pick up from my box?" customers will ask. A prepared banker would explain:

I can appreciate the work involved in organizing your internal collections system and your not wanting to modify this system unless there were substantial advantages to you. I would like to learn a little more about your system to determine what advantages may exist for you.

How often do you presently collect your remittances? I think that you will find that there will be significant advantages to you in utilizing our Lock Box. We will pick up your mail 8 times through a twenty-four-hour period. Our Lock Box has a unique zip code that can accelerate the delivery of remittances by reducing mail float (the time it takes a payment to reach its destination) and thereby can improve your cash flow. What are your thoughts on the advantages of utilizing our unique zip code to accelerate your cash flow?

To qualify for a Lock Box, a customer is required to use the bank's number. By understanding the qualifying criteria and the reason for it, bankers can cooperate with operations, and at the same time satisfy customer needs and concerns.

Sometimes bankers, in their enthusiasm to meet customer needs, agree to options that place unnecessary burdens on the operations and service area and may reduce the quality of the service to the customer. This frequently results in internal difficulties for the operations area, dissatisfaction from the customer who does not receive what he or she thought had been purchased, and strained relations between operations and the line. By understanding the criteria and capabilities of a product, bankers can increase external as well as internal satisfaction.

In addition to creating a satisfactory relationship between customers and the bank, and between bankers and the operations area of the bank, attention to qualifying criteria is an important time-management, prospecting, and cross-selling tool. Spending time with false prospects is expensive and unproductive for both bankers and their customers. Understanding qualifying criteria can assist bankers in separating "suspects" from prospects and thereby save and maximize time. Qualifying criteria can also help customer relations, since bankers who have inaccurate or incomplete qualifying criteria can convey a poor image for the bank or even damage a relationship by having to back out of a sale and reject a customer after initiating the discussion. For example, a banker may interest a customer in a Lock Box only to find out that he or she does not have the required number of mailed remittances. Qualifying criteria can also help bankers identify cross-selling opportunities with present customers, or enable them to substitute products when customers don't qualify for a particular product.

Qualifying criteria revolve around three critical considerations:

1   Is the customer eligible for a particular product?
2   Does the product satisfy the customer's needs?
3   Can the banker effect a mutually beneficial relationship between the customer and the bank?

Qualifying criteria help bankers match the product with the customer. In determining if the product and the customer complement one another, bankers should consider:

The specific qualifying criteria for the product.
The eligibility of the customer.

The customer's needs.

The responsiveness of the product to the customer's needs.

The decision-maker's understanding of this need.

Benefit to the customer.

Profitability for the bank.

Understanding the specific qualifying criteria of a product will enable bankers to identify prospects and initiate discussions.

Customer Contact

To be more effective and to save time, bankers should direct their sales efforts to the decision-maker or the decision-influencer. They should have information concerning the appropriate position to be contacted for specific products. In discussing Foreign Exchange, bankers should set appointments with the treasurer, foreign exchange manager, or the international cash manager, depending on the organization of the company. For Certificates of Deposit, bankers should probably see an investment officer, portfolio manager, treasurer, or an individual investor. Although the treasurer seems to be a common thread for most bank products, it is important that the identity of key decision-makers be known. In developing their contacts, bankers should remember to develop "depth contacts" by meeting with the high (economic) decision-makers, and the wide (user) decision-makers. Establishing "high and wide" contacts helps ensure support and minimizes internal undermining in the company based on misinformation, fear, or politics! (See pages 120–122 for a discussion of High and Wide Selling.)

Representative Customers

Bankers should be given the names, industry, and location of satisfied customers who are using the product. Bankers can refer to the companies to build customer confidence as well as their own. Although specific contact names in the company may not be used, it is advisable to secure permission from the companies to use their names as references. Products for whom the clients are confidential such as Personal Trust or Factoring should not be listed and an explanation about the confidential nature of the product should be explained to the banker.

Probing Questions

Bankers should be given specific probing questions for each product to assist them in opening their product discussions, in qualifying a customer, and in uncovering needs. The probing questions should be open ended, requiring more than a yes or no reply. Probing questions are an excellent way to interest the customer in the sales interview since they involve him or her in the sale. Probing questions are the questions that product specialists, and other seasoned bankers based on their years of experience, know to be effective in initiating a sale, and by providing them to bankers, the bank can accelerate their sales effectiveness. (See pages 51–55 for a discussion of Probing Questions.)

Objections and Responses

Almost all of the objections concerning a particular product or a particular bank have been voiced. Bankers with sales experience in a particular product are familiar with and prepared for the objections raised by customers. Bankers should, whenever possible, be prepared for inherent objections and should construct the basis of the responses *before* meeting with the customer. When bankers have anticipated the objections that experience demonstrates are likely to be raised, they are better prepared to stay in the sale, complete the sale, or make a qualified referral to the specialists. (See pages 65–90 for a complete discussion of Objections.)

Competitive Information

To maximize sales opportunities, bankers should have information on their *competitor's products as well as their own.* Competitive information enables bankers to point out (and create) their product advantages. An understanding of the competitor's product is the key to carving out a competitive edge among products that *appear* to be similar. Without competitive information, bankers cannot compare their competitor's strengths and weaknesses with their bank's competitive selling points. Because competitive information is not easily gathered, bankers can be susceptible to customer pressures about competitive offers or rumors or misperceptions about their own product's failings. The three key ingredients for selling are one's own product knowledge, competitive knowledge, and customer knowledge. Without competitive information bankers cannot answer objections concerning "other offers," nor can they appreciate their own bank's capabilities. Bankers should know who their major competitors are and also the "trade" names for the competitor's products.

Following is an example of competitive information:

Product: Check Reconcilement

Competitive Strength	Competitive Weaknesses	Our Competitive Selling Points
	X Bank	
Volume over 500 items (ours is 1,000 items)	Use purchased hardware, therefore is less flexible	Offer four different reports
	More errors	Personal service from account officer who
Offers check retention or check destruction	Higher price for options	stays involved as liaison
More branches		Manual and automated
		Competitive item charge
		Prompt turnaround (complete reconcilement in seven days)
		Our own in-house system, which is more flexible
	Y Bank	
More branches	Small, inexperienced staff	Experienced staff
Flexible in-house system		Total cash management consulting capabilities

Although specific competitive information is very difficult to gather, bankers should have specific information on all of their major competitors if they are to help customers compare price and value. Competitive information is a two-way street; it should be provided by the bank to the bankers and also from line bankers to product or divisional management. (See Feedback Summary, page 27.) Of course, it is unprofessional to use competitive information in a derogatory or maligning way. Competitive information should be used to help customers make objective comparisons.

Case History

Case histories are useful in documenting customer benefits by providing an example of the product in action. In presenting a case history bankers should discuss the situation or problem that existed, the bank action that corrected the problem, and the customer benefits in terms of time savings, efficiency, accuracy, peace of mind, and dollars.

Action Step

Bankers should be familiar with the different action steps for products marketed in their area. The action step is the first step in implementing the product. It should be used to conclude the meeting and to *establish the next step* as a way to get the ball rolling. Action steps turn "hello calls" into sales calls. Action steps will vary according to the type and complexity of the product and the customer's situation, but can range from setting an appointment with a specialist to completing the sale. For example:

> When would it be convenient for a cash management specialist to contact you to discuss a Lock Box study to determine the most efficient way to process your remittances?

Setting a specific action step is the responsibility of the banker. Possible action steps should be planned *prior* to making the sales call. (See pages 95-97 Action Step.)

Implementation Process

Bankers should know the steps that *they,* the *customer,* and the *specialists* must take to get the customer on board and to implement the product. Implementation steps include qualifying the prospect, gathering data, introducing the product specialists or the technical person, seeking and attaining internal approvals (if credit-related), and arranging for and completing all operational testing procedures and signing of documents. For example, one step of the implementation process for Foreign Exchange Service would be: Calling officer makes recommendation to Credit Committee that an unconfirmed foreign exchange line be extended to the customer. The implementation process should clearly define *who, when, where, how,* and in *what order* each step occurs.

Operational Process

Bankers should also be aware of the *follow-up* operational procedures and activities that take place during the life of the product after the customer has signed up. By understanding the operational procedures, bankers can assist the customer if there are problems and can respond to questions concerning service or delivery. For example, one step of the operating procedures for Letters of Credit would be: Letters of Credit Department notifies applicant if there are discrepancies in the documents and makes payment advices . . .

Pricing

Pricing is a critical feature of a product. Bankers should be aware of the fees and balances for a particular product, the fee parameter, and situations that require input from the technical specialists to determine pricing. Bankers should remember that price is a feature of the product, and when discussing price they should treat it like any feature by linking it with its benefits. Pricing information is critical, and bankers should not be deprived of it because it is may be negotiated based on options or the relationship. Bankers should be given pricing parameters, and instructions to defer price to specialists when the pricing requires input from the specialists. Many banks are rethinking their pricing structure to determine the profitability of the non-credit and credit related products. Management should conduct pricing studies, make pricing and marketing determinations and provide bankers with pricing and marketing rationale. For example for Foreign Exchange:

Pricing

Market rates which change minute to minute. No additional charge. . . .

Profitability

Profit comes from spread between purchase and sale price.

Marketing Rationale

Enhances bank's image as full service bank. Opportunity to cross sell. . . .
Strengthens relationship. (See pages 70 to 76 for discussion on Pricing.)

In-Bank Contact

Bankers should be given the names and extensions of in-bank specialists to
be contacted for additional product information. Access to specialists is important if bankers are to make referrals or have their questions answered.

Start-Up Time

Customers almost always want to know how long it will take to begin, and
bankers should know how long it takes to get a product operational. If
volume or complexity make start-up time indefinite, bankers should be
given the time parameters, since efficient and timely start-up time can be a
strong competitive selling point. One regional bank got substantial (and
long-term) Import Letter of Credit business from a national company
because it could approve the line and implement the service in one and a
half days.

Agreements and Contracts

Bankers should be familiar with the documents or contracts that must be
signed and the forms to be completed to ensure smooth implementation.
They should be prepared to explain any complex or unique agreements such
as the loan agreement for Master Notes.

Cross-Sell Alert

Bankers should be aware of the relationship among the bank's products and
use the sale of one product as a hinge to sell other related or sometimes
unrelated products that satisfy the customer's needs or improve his or her
situation. For example, a company that uses Import Letter of Credit may be
an excellent candidate for Foreign Exchange, and a company that uses Account Reconcilement may be an excellent candidate for Balance Reporting.

Product Family

Often a particular product fits into a product area, and bankers should have an understanding of this. For example, Depository Transfer Checks is a product in the Cash Management Area. The product family consists of:

Cash Management

Collections	Disbursements	Cash Reporting Control
Concentration Accounts	Account Reconcilement	Balance Reporting
Depository Transfer Checks	Controlled Disbursements	
Lock Box	Money Transfers	
Wire Transfers	Payable through Drafts	
	Zero Balance Account	

Exhibits

It is helpful for bankers to have convenient access to brochures, sample letters, advertisements, or other materials relevant to the product. (See pages 122–127, Sales Materials.)

Feedback from the Field

The nineteen categories discussed so far represent information directed from the specialists or operations area to the line bankers. Just as management should see to it that product information is channeled on an ongoing basis to bankers, it should encourage the flow of communication from the field to the specialists. The specialists have a great deal of product information about the bank's own products, and bankers who have day-to-day, face-to-face contact with customers frequently have a great deal of information about competitive products and market trends and demands. Because of their customer contact, they are often aware of market developments and competitive changes *before* specialists or management. When management does not tap this source of market information, it loses the opportunity to identify market trends, initiate product advancements, and make pricing or product adjustments.

Compiling data about key competitors is not simple, and since bankers are the ones who have bits and pieces from their customers, their information must be pooled if a clear competitive picture is to be developed. Open communication between line bankers and product specialists or operations is very important if market opportunities are to be seized. Unless bankers channel competitive information concerning product advantages and product disadvantages to their managers, the bank will not be in a position to respond to changes and demands and will not have the information necessary to improve a particular product, disseminate competitive data, or correct bankers' own in-house misperceptions about their product.

All information from the field is of great importance in the marketing effort. Too often it is bankers' own misperceptions about their product's "inferiority" that is more detrimental and dangerous to the sale of the product than competitors themselves, and such misperceptions should be corrected if market share is to be maintained. There are various ways in which bankers can communicate important competitive information, such as sales meetings and product seminars. Too often, however, vital information is lost over coffee or in a passing comment. Managers should encourage bankers to consistently and systematically feed back in-the-field information. To facilitate centralizing competitive information, bankers should submit their feedback to their managers, and managers should forward the hard data or hearsay and all other information to the appropriate areas. By systematically channeling information into the bank and by verifying and sharing the researched information, bankers can not only multiply the benefits of their sales experience but also contribute to effecting product improvements.

A feedback form that can be placed at the end of each individual profile or a Feedback Tablet that could be given to bankers are effective ways to collect and monitor information from the field. The feedback should be used to relay the following kinds of information:

Competitive information (pricing, service, capabilities).

Product disadvantages and advantages (verified or perceived).

Objections.

Additional customer benefits.

Comments or suggestions.

The feedback forms should be submitted to managers and researched by the unit that develops and disseminates product information in conjunction with the specialists.

Feedback Form

Exhibit 1   Sample Feedback Form

Name of Product: _____ Date: _____

Information on Competitors (pricing, service, capabilities, market thrust, market penetration, new customers, changes in product, marketing brochures)

_____

_____

_____

_____

Competitive Disadvantages and Advantages for Our Product (bankers' or customers' perceptions—rumors or hard data)

_____

_____

_____

_____

Additional Objections, Probing Questions, Benefits

_____

_____

_____

_____

Comments or Suggestions

_____

_____

Source of Information or Situation (optional)

_____

Signature _____ Ext. _____ Date _____

Please forward to: _____

SALES LINE

The alternative to providing bankers with the twenty critical categories of sales information on their key products is to have them miss countless opportunities to sell and cross-sell. The following line represents a *sale*:

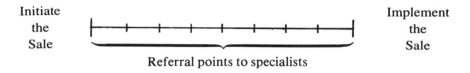

The twenty categories of product information are designed to help bankers *get on* and *stay on* the sales line. Without adequate product knowledge, they cannot get on and cannot stay on! The categories are designed to provide bankers with information that is comprehensive but not overwhelming. Depending on the complexity of the product, bankers are expected to advance to a particular stage in the sale. Not providing bankers with viable product information is costly in *lost opportunities* and lost sales. Without such information, bankers may never have the opportunity to advance in the sale or to make a referral to a specialist.

For those who think twenty categories may be too much information, it is important to reflect on the objectives of disseminating product information. Bankers are being asked to *initiate* business. These categories will provide them with the kind of information they need to confidently initiate sales calls and successfully complete them. Bankers need this kind of information on the range of products marketed in their area. Without adequate sales-oriented product information on a *range* of products, bankers will be unable to recognize or capitalize on the signals sent directly or indirectly by customers during a sales interview. Adequate product knowledge can assist bankers in increasing the selling and cross-selling of credit and noncredit products.

Developing this kind of product information may seem time consuming, but in the long run it is really time saving. Unless bankers have five to ten years (as they did in the past) to become seasoned by going the rounds of the organization, they should have convenient access to up-to-date sales oriented product information on all products relevant in their market area as a way to accelerate their development, support them in their sales activities, and increase their individual productivity.

Bankers need a centralized source of up-to-date comprehensive product information, and the individual profile format is an excellent way to provide it. Bankers, the specialists, and the bank benefit by such a system because of the increase in quality referrals and the resulting opportunity to increase market share.

PRODUCT KNOWLEDGE QUESTIONS

Bankers with cross-selling responsibilities can make sure they have sufficient information on each product marketed in their area by considering the following questions *before* initiating cross-selling discussions with customers:

What is the product and how does it work?

How does the product tie into a customer's needs or situation?

What are the primary features and benefits of each product?

What are the qualifying criteria for customer eligibility?

Who are some customers who use this product?

Who is the decision-maker?

What probing questions should be asked to uncover needs and qualifications and lead into the discussion to interest the customer?

What objections are likely to be raised? What are the main points to use in resolving the objections?

What action should be taken at the conclusion of the meeting as a firm next step?

Who is the primary competition in this area?

What is an appropriate case history?

What is the pricing structure?

Who is the specialist for the product or the in-bank contact for additional information?

How long does it take to get started once an agreement to use the product or service is reached?

What are the operational procedures (before and after signatures)?

What materials, brochures, and further data are available?

The following list outlines the wide range of products that can be provided by commercial banks. Products with an asterisk are the more commonly marketed products.

Representative Product List:
Commercial Products

Acceptance Financing*

Automated Payroll*

Asset Based Financing (Accounts Receivable Financing, Inventory, Equipment)

Account Reconciliation Plan*

A Forfait Financing

Bank Safekeeping

Balance Reporting*

Bankers Acceptances*

Cash Letters* (Domestic, International)

Credit Line

Custodian Service

Certificates of Deposit*

Commercial Loans*

Commercial Checking Accounts*

Commercial Paper* (Investment, Issuance, Agency)

Commercial Finance (Asset Based Financing)

Corporate Bond Services (Registrar, Paying Agent, Transfer Agent)

Corporate Stock Services

Corporate Savings Accounts*

Corporate Trustee*—Indenture

Corporate Finance Advisory

Coupon Collection/Cremation

Custody of Securities*

Depository Transfer Checks*

Direct Deposit Payroll* (Automated Clearing House Payments)

Direct Lending*

Divestitures

Documentary Drafts

Employee Benefit Plan (record keeping)

Employee Stock Option Plan Purchase and Dividend (ESOP)

Escrow Services

Equipment Finance

Eurobond Financing

Eurobond Purchase and Sale

Eurocurrency Syndicated Loans

Eurodollar Deposit

Executorship*

Eximbank

Export Financing (Eximbank, Hermes, COFACE, etc.)

Factoring (Commercial Finance)

Federal Funds*—Purchase and Sales*

Foreign Accounts Receivable Financing

Foreign Collections—Inward and Outward*

Foreign Exchange Advisory

Foreign Exchange Trading (Foreign Currency)*

Foreign Remittances

Industrial Sales Finance (Vendor Financing)

International Cash Management Products*

International Paying and Receiving

Investment Advisory

Investment Counseling*

Investment Management*

Letters of Credit
    Import*
    Export*
    Standby
    Documentary
    Reimbursement (banks)

Lock Box* (Wholesale and Retail)

Leverage Leasing

Master Trust

Master Notes

Municipal Notes and Bonds

Payable Through Drafts*
Paying Agent for Municipal Bonds
Peer Trusts
Pension Plan Portfolio Management
Pre-Authorized Checks
Private Placement
Project Financing
Payroll Processing
Repurchase Agreements
Retirement Benefit Plans
Safekeeping (Depository Trust Company)*
Securities Collections
Self-Employed Benefit Plans*
Short-Term Tax Exempts
Tax Exempt Municipal Bonds
Testamentary Trusts
Term Loans (Secured, Unsecured)
Transfer Agent
True Lease:
    International
    Leverage Investor
    Single Investor
Trustee Under a Will
U.S. Dollar Clearing
U.S. Treasury Bills and Notes
Wire Transfers*
Zero Balance Accounts*

Representative Consumer Banking Products

Auto Leasing
Auto Loan
Automated Teller Machine
Automated Transfer Service
Automobile Loans

Bank by Mail
Certificates of Deposit
Certified Checks
Checking Accounts
Collections
Coupon Collections
Direct Deposit of Payroll, Dividends, Social Security
Foreign Currency or Foreign Exchange
High Interest Savings
Holiday Club
Home Improvement Loans
Individual Retirement Accounts
Investment Management
Keogh Plans
Line of Credit—Personal
Liquid-loophole Certificate
Master Charge
Merchant Banking
Money Market Instruments
Money Orders
Mortgages
NOW Accounts
Overdraft
Pay by Phone
Payroll Deduction
Personal Line of Credit
Personal Loan
Point of Sales
Pre-Authorized Payments
Regular Checking Account
Regular (Passbook) Savings
Savings Certificates
Safe Deposit Boxes
Safe Keeping
Statement Savings

Tax-Free Certificates
(All Savers)

Student Loans

Telephone Transfer

Travelers Checks

Trust Services

Utility Payments

U.S. Savings Bonds

VISA

TYING PRODUCT KNOWLEDGE WITH CUSTOMER NEEDS

Customers make financial decisions every day. Bankers who understand their customers' objectives, constraints, problems, and priorities and their bank's products or services can recommend alternatives, promote their bank's products, and satisfy customer needs. Unless bankers understand their customer's needs, they risk making presentations that are of little or no interest to their customers.

Bankers cannot satisfy their customers' needs without understanding them. Since those needs are not always *immediately* visible bankers must use research and the *sales interview itself* to identify and confirm needs. Developing customer knowledge is often time consuming and difficult. The bank's market research department, a company's annual report, financial report resources such as Dun and Bradstreet, and other customers can provide bankers with valuable customer information prior to the sales call. Since financial sources such as Dun and Bradstreet may be outdated or inaccurate, they should be supplemented and checked for accuracy. If up-to-date resources are not available, bankers should call company switchboards to confirm names, titles, or ask for information concerning the organization. Sometimes important information can be gathered from a conversation with the switchboard or a secretary. Developing customer information requires that bankers be resourceful; bankers should develop their customer knowledge if they intend to satisfy customer needs.

Bankers should gather as many of the following data as possible about a customer *prior* to making sales calls:

What is the company's business (wholesale, retail, manufacturer, etc.)?

Who is the chief financial officer?

Who is the most appropriate contact in the company?

Who is the decision maker? Who else should the banker meet with? (Bankers tend to call on senior management but they often should also meet with operational personnel, etc.)

How long has the company been in business?

What is the size of the company (annual sales volume, number of employees, or net worth)?

Where is the company located (county, town, city, zip code)?

What is the type of organization (headquarters, subsidiary)?

How does it compare in the industry (reputation with trade, customers, competition)?

What is the customer's relationship with the bank?

What are the customer's goals and objectives?

What are the customer's constraints?

What difficulties, concerns, or needs does the customer have?

Is there a third-party referral?

Sales Interview Fact-Finding

Information that cannot be gathered in advance of the sales interview should be gathered immediately before and during the sales call. While waiting to see their customers, bankers might read annual reports or other in-house literature, talk to support personnel, and observe the business environment and the business facility. More importantly, bankers *should use the sales interview* to discover facts, test assumptions, and identify customer needs. By asking *questions* in a positive and consultative manner, bankers can learn important information about their customers. Early in the sales interview, bankers should find out how a customer is presently handling particular aspects of his or her business and how satisfactory the present system is. They should be prepared with specific back-up questions to determine areas in which the customer's present systems can be complemented or improved.

A word of caution to bankers is to give some information to the customer before asking questions too early. A brief introduction, a brief summary of events leading to the meeting, a statement of general objective, and hint of a possible benefit all provide excellent leads into questions about the customer's needs and interests. By asking questions in a positive and con-sultative manner bankers can identify what the customer is presently doing or considering. Bankers often do not ask enough questions; hence they don't uncover customer problems or gain insight into their customers' plans or objectives.

Testing Assumptions

Questions are also useful in testing the validity of assumptions. When bankers meet with their customers they usually have a set of assumptions concerning the customers' needs and their sales topic. The assumptions should be based on homework and the banker's own experience with a par-ticular industry or customer. Making assumptions is a necessary part of planning for the sales call; it is important, however, for bankers to remember that assumptions are educated guesses, which must be tested, modified, or confirmed, before or during the sales interview, before action is taken on them.

By testing assumptions with probing questions, bankers usually can pro-ceed with confidence that they are addressing the needs and concerns of the customer. Bankers who take the time to develop assumptions in their sales planning stage and to test them before engaging in a product discussion are likely to hit on topics of interest and be in a position to key in on products or alternatives that are relevant to the customer. A discussion of a product should come *after* the customers' needs are identified. Product knowledge, homework, and probing questions are the key tools in developing customer knowledge; the products discussed by bankers should be selected from their pool of product information as they respond to the customer's situation.

SUMMARY

Product knowledge is the foundation of sales. Bankers should understand their products from a sales perspective, and they should link their product knowledge to their customer's needs. The more information bankers have about their products and their customers, the more likely they are to recognize and bring out needs, develop viable solutions, and meld the prod-uct with the customer.

3
Consultative Sales Approach

TEN ELEMENTS OF A SALES INTERVIEW

Observation and participation in sales situations indicate that certain elements consistently occur during successful sales interviews. By understanding these elements it is possible for bankers to conduct more successful sales interviews on a consistent basis.

Ten elements of a sale were identified in role play and in field experiences with more than one thousand bankers. By applying them regularly during their sales interviews, bankers can increase their effectiveness. Although the following ten elements are isolated into ten distinct categories for discussion purposes, they are not independent of one another, and they do not occur in a vacuum or in a fixed sequence in an actual sales situation.

The ten elements that consistently occur during successful consultative sales are:

1 *Opening:*

   Greetings and introduction.

   Breaking the ice (optional).

   Summary.

   Selling the interview (objective and possible benefit).

   Bridge question.

2 *Customer Motivation Lever:* identifying the customer's primary needs and concerns.

3 *Probing questions:* using open-ended questions to qualify the customer or uncover needs.

4. *Constructive listening:* paying attention to and *using* what the customer says.

5. *Features and Benefits:* linking features with customer benefits.

6. *Fielding objections:* anticipating and responding to objections.

7. *Incremental close:* testing for agreement and understanding throughout the sales interview.

8. *Action step:* initiating the first step of the implementation process.

9. *Body signals:* using nonverbal communication to support, supple-

ment, or evaluate what is verbally communicated.

10 *Sales environment:* observing the setting for the sale and its impact on the sale.

With the exception of the opening, customer's Motivation Lever, and action step, which should be kept in sequence, all of the other elements are interspersed throughout the sales call. The opening and action step are stationary for obvious reasons, and the Motivation Lever, although not so stationary, must be uncovered before a discussion of a specific product begins.

An effective sales interview is a fluid, living encounter, rather than a series of programmed steps or a preset sequence. Bankers can be hit with an objection or question immediately as during the opening. Certainly they should respond to the customer, but awareness of the ten elements allows them to return to the opening after they have addressed the customer's concern without rushing into a product discussion before the customer's needs are identified and understood by both the banker *and* the customer. In this way bankers can maintain control of the course of the sales interview. By understanding that they must identify needs and stimulate interest before they attempt to sell a product, bankers can avoid having customers control the sale by rushing them in and out of topics. They can also avoid the "laundry list" trap of reciting products that are of little or no interest to the customer.

Although the time frame, mix, formality, or comprehensiveness of each of the ten elements may vary from product to product, customer to customer, industry to industry, banker to banker, or relationship to relationship, the ten elements should be a part of *every* sale. These elements provide a blueprint of the consultative selling process. By understanding them, bankers can individualize their sales interviews and develop a professional style that is effective with a wide range of customers. Bankers should not try to function as chameleons. Although sensitivity and responsiveness to individual customer styles are essential, bankers should strive to develop *one* professional approach. Although there are a number of approaches that bankers can use, the ten-elements approach increases bankers' ability to complete successful sales calls with a wide range of customers and in a variety of situations.

By understanding the sales process, bankers can increase their awareness of what is taking place and can control and manage what transpires. Bankers who understand their products from their customer's point of view, encourage customer input, and satisfy customer concerns and objections can be in control of the sales interview. Unfortunately, the word "control" often has a negative connotation. Control is essential during the sales interview—not overbearing, dominant, and inflexible control but flexible control in which bankers adjust the sales interview to the customer's needs. Bankers should assume the leadership role during the sales discussion, if they expect to have a role in formulating the buy decisions. They should not be pushed through the interview like a cork at sea but rather should channel and guide the sales discussion.

By utilizing the ten elements, bankers can pace the presentation, delay discussing topics that are premature or are a separate issue, or *consciously* direct the conversation to respond to needs as they emerge. An understanding of the sales process reduces the number of occasions in which bankers ask themselves *after* the sales interview, "What went wrong?"

The ten elements are designed to help bankers conclude mutually beneficial relationships in situations in which their products are a viable alternative and are basically competitive in price and quality. The ten elements also assist bankers in selling superior products by assuring that customers recognize and appreciate the product's superiority. No matter how excellent a product is, an ineffective sales interview can destroy the sales opportunity. The ten-element approach does not come with a 100% guarantee. It can, however, increase the number of successful calls because it assists BANKERS in identifying and satisfying customer needs.

The ten elements offer an approach for leading consultative sales interviews. All bank products have their strengths and weaknesses. It is the bankers' ability to differentiate their own products and *communicate the value* of the product relative to customer *needs* that distinguishes products, bankers, and banks. *Bankers' ability to understand and discuss their products from the customer's point of view is one of the primary ways in which product differentiation can be established and accepted by customers.* Bankers are the bank's most important asset. Bankers who can help customers make decisions with confidence provide their bank and themselves with a competitive edge in profitably expanding their market share in an increasingly aggressive marketplace. The ten elements assist bankers in establishing a sales environment in which the customer's needs, objectives, constraints, and priorities can be identified and satisfied. Each of the ten elements is designed to develop and maintain a dialogue between bankers and their customers. The following sections examine each of the ten elements and their application in selling situations.

Opening

The Importance of the Opening

The opening sets the tone for the sales call. It is during the opening that bankers should establish a consultative approach. The objective of the opening is to prepare the customer for the sales interview—to make the customer receptive to the sales call.

In consultative banking the opening is more than the greeting; it is actually the overture of the sales call, in which bankers prepare the customer by focusing on what is in the sales interview for the customer rather than focusing on the product or the bank's objectives. Since the impact of the opening far outweighs the brief amount of time it takes to open, it may be helpful to examine how to maximize the first few minutes of the sales call.

Parts of a Consultative Opening

By understanding the purpose and content of the opening, bankers can feel more confident initiating calls with new and old customers alike. There are five distinct activities that should be a part of every opening:

Greeting and Introductions.   Depending on the nature of the relationship, the formality and length of time dedicated to the greeting and the introduction will vary. The introduction includes name of banker, name of bank, presentation of business cards, and so on. Judgment should come into play in determining the content and formality of the introduction; however, with the new customer, it is suggested that the titles Mr., Miss, or Mrs. be used until the customer suggests a first-name basis. Bankers who *assume* first-name liberties relinquish the opportunity for the customer to give a signal of rapport by suggesting a first-name basis. Also with a customer who may not be familiar with the bank or the banker, the location of the bank and a brief description of the bank and the banker's position is appropriate.

Ice Breaking or Warm-Up (optional).   Ice breaking refers to discussing topics that are not directly related to the objective of the sales call. Many bankers can utilize items of personal interest such as a painting or trophy to break the ice. Some bankers utilize the location, the trip, or a sports team as a warm-up. It is usually advisable to keep ice breaking brief and business-related, such as commenting on an attractive new facility, a civic award, or perhaps the lovely countryside in the area. This warm-up period is often more appropriate and more successful with customers with whom rapport has been established and personal interests have been identified, rather than with new customers on prospect calls. Ice breaking with new customers can be risky, since it requires making presumptions about opinions, interests, and values. Thus, ice breaking should be handled with care. Bankers must exercise judgment in deciding whether or not to break the ice and should take cultural and geographic customs into consideration. This is the *optional* part of the opening, which can be utilized by bankers as they deem appropriate.

Summary.   After the greeting, introduction, and the optional ice breaking, bankers should be prepared to briefly *summarize the events that led to the meeting.* The summary can briefly recap a former meeting, or refer to the events that brought about the meeting such as a third-party referral, an article in the paper, a new shopping center, a new branch of the bank, a new product, a change in organizational structure (bank's or customer's), or the telephone call that led to the appointment. The summary should lead into the *most important* part of the opening, the *selling of the sales interview.*

Selling the Idea of the Interview.   After the summary bankers should make a general statement concerning why they are there and help set the focus of the meeting. The *general objectives* should be set prior to making the call. Particularly on first calls the objective should be broad, such as determining customer requirements. If there is a lead, the objective can be more targeted, such as discussing cash management with a customer with a large number of mailed remittances. Bankers can sell the interview by linking the objective of the call *with the possible benefits* to the customer.

Selling the interview serves to motivate the customer to participate in the meeting. Customers are motivated to participate when they perceive:

1   An opportunity to improve their situation by increasing profits, improving operations through new technology, changing their image, solving probings, or satisfying personal agendas.

2   An opportunity to avoid risk or loss.

3   A dissatisfaction with their current situation.

Unless customers perceive the possibility of one or more of these situations right from the start, they will not have the incentive to participate actively in the sales interview.

Bankers who sell the idea of the interview help the customer recognize the possible benefits that can accrue from the discussion. Of course the benefits should be general to allow for flexibility in the sales interview. Selling the idea of the interview is accomplished by discussing the possible benefits that the customer may derive from a particular product or service. Bankers should hint at the benefits that are likely to be of interest to the customer. They should avoid exaggerated claims or overstatements during the selling of the interview stage to keep expectations at a realistic level and to establish credibility.

Bankers who sell the interview before selling a product are able to generate customer interest and involvement and capture the attention of the customer. Bankers who do not take the time to sell the idea of the interview may never succeed in getting the sales interview off the ground. They may find themselves midway through the call still looking for a topic or product that will spark customer interest. After selling the idea of the interview bankers use the bridge question to enter into the Motivation Lever segment of the sale.

Bridge Question.   Bankers bridge from the Opening to the "Motivation Lever" segment of the sales interview by asking a question *that is designed to encourage the customer to talk about his or her situation.* The question should be based on the banker's research or experience with the customer, the industry, the product, or the bank's capabilities. Bankers should prepare their primary questions as well as some back-up questions to use with less responsive customers to encourage their input. The bridge question leads into the second element of the sale, the Motivation Lever.

The following is an example of a consultative opening:

Banker.	Good morning Mr. Wilson. I'm Tom Alster with X Bank in Philadelphia. I am with the National Division and our bank has a strong commitment to. . . . I appreciated the opportunity to speak with you on Tuesday and your taking the time to meet with me today. As we discussed, X Bank has developed a flexible cash management system that is being utilized by a number of companies in your	Greeting and introduction summary Objective

industry, which may be of value to you in. . . .

Before going into details about our capabilities,   Bridge
it would be helpful if you could tell me a little   question
about the movement of cash in your company.

How are you currently collecting your remit-   Back-up
tance?   questions

How satisfied are you with the availability of
. . .?

How do you fund your dispersement accounts?

How do you get your balance information?

Customer.   As we handle it now, . . .

The five opening activities, greeting and introduction, ice breaking, summary, selling the interview, and the bridge question provide bankers with an
organized and individual way to open the sales call. Although bankers'
words, style, and mannerisms must be their own and vary according to the
situation, the structure of the opening should remain the same. Although
the content should vary, the process should not. The result is not a canned
opening as in programmed or door-to-door selling, but rather a professional opening based on preparation. The objective of the five parts of the
opening is to increase bankers' confidence and effectiveness in initiating
business, and to help them to consistently open in a positive manner. The
structure is polite, constructive, consultative, and realistic. Like other professionals, when bankers have an awareness of the process and have a plan
for openings, they can exercise greater control over what takes place.

On prospecting calls, bankers are required to spend more on the introduction and the selling of the interview. In subsequent meetings the focus shifts
to the summary of the last meeting and checking with the customer on the
status of conditions, interests, problems, and developments since the last
meeting.

By understanding the opening process, bankers can confidently and professionally initiate the sales interview. Even with customers who begin to
complain or object immediately after the greeting, bankers are better able to
retain control of the sales interview. Bankers can listen to the customer's
point of view, explanation, or problems, respond to what the customer has
said, and *then go back to the part of the opening that was interrupted.* This
sharp focus enables bankers to exercise control early in the sales interview

and therefore exercise greater control over the sales results.

Strategies for Opening

The following strategies can be used by bankers to strengthen their openings during the summary or selling of the interview stage.

The Customer Benefit Strategy.   The hint of a benefit should be a part of *every* opening as an invitation for the customer's attention. By suggesting the possibility of greater profits, improved service, or avoidance of a possible loss, bankers can gain the customer's attention. The *benefit strategy* requires that bankers know something about the customer's business, situation, and needs. For instance, a customer (the owner of a large gift shop) who uses numerous Letters of Credits may be interested in consolidating them, reducing costs, and simplifying internal clerical in-house procedures. The benefits should be presented as *possibilities* that will be determined by the customer's situation and needs. Benefit openings should be low-key selling in which the words "may" and "possibly" are used to replace the exaggerated claims or sweeping statements that can cause customers to doubt bankers' credibility and cause them to retreat. A customer benefit opening transforms "I would like to discuss our Import Letter of Credit service" to "I'd like to discuss the possible ways in which we may be able to improve your turnaround time. . ." Benefit opening strategy shifts the focus of the opening from the bank's capabilities to the customer's needs and situation.

Professional Compliment Strategy.   By doing their homework, bankers can utilize the compliment strategy to demonstrate interest and appreciation of the customer and his or her business. Professional compliments should be sincere, accurate, timely, and individualized if they are to be meaningful. An example of a professional compliment opening would be a reference to a new acquisition or an industry award.

Third-Party Strategy.   Having a third-party referral is perhaps the most positive way to begin an interview. Bankers who are introduced or referred by a third party have a substantial advantage. They can make use of these referrals to get in the door; once there, they should establish a rapport and when necessary utilize their first contact to gain an introduction or access to other decision-makers or to the appropriate decision-maker.

Hinge Strategy.   By using any mutual point of reference to create a connection with the customer, bankers can help establish common ground. A *hinge* can be anything from a letter sent by the banker, an article in the paper, or a mutual acquaintance.

Customer Experience Strategy.   This strategy is a kind of professional name-dropping. By referring to a company that is similar in size and type of business, which is respected in the industry, bankers can earn the customer's attention and demonstrate that they have a working knowledge of the customer's business. This strategy is particularly useful in meeting with customers who are not familiar with the bank or a particular product. When using specific company names, bankers should secure permission for using the company as a reference, prior to using them. Bankers should take care to use the names to build confidence, not to imply "me-tooism."

The Question Strategy.   The questioning opening is the bridge into the second element of the sale. The bridge question should be a part of every opening. Initial questioning should be handled gently, rather than like a prosecuting attorney. After bankers have given some information (greeting and introduction, ice breaking, summary, and selling the idea of the interview) they should ask permission to ask some questions to better understand the customer's situation. These questions are most important in understanding the customer's point of view and frame of reference. It is important for bankers to use their questions to involve the customer and find out what is on his or her mind so that bankers can address topics that are relevant.

An example of a consultative opening utilizing a third-party referral, a benefit, and a bridge question is:

> Mr. Jones, I'm Tom Smith, X Bank. I appreciated the opportunity to speak with you last week. My discussion with John Williams, at your headquarters, indicated that you may be interested in looking at some alternative ways to collect your remittances to improve your cash flow. *Before discussing how an alternative method may assist you in paying down your loans, it would be helpful if you might describe how you currently collect your remittances.*

Highly successful sales people use the bridge question as the key to the entire sale.

Multiple Openings

During a sales call, bankers are often introduced to other individuals in the same company immediately after meeting with their first contact. Bankers who find themselves faced with a series of meetings on the same subject back to back should remember to "open" each time! Whether the second meeting is with a corporate treasurer, a partner, or a family member, bankers should remember to reopen with each new contact. If bankers assume that their first opening will *automatically transfer* to the next person, they may find themselves discussing matters that threaten, overwhelm, confuse, or bore the customer. Regardless of how many individuals they meet, they should repeat, even if in a capsulized form, the introduction, summary, and selling the idea of the interview and bridge question before they begin a product discussion. The summary of the initial meeting and checking for agreement is essential during miniopenings. Too many "in the bag" sales are lost because of a failure to reopen with new decision-makers!

Tone

The tone of the opening will influence the entire sales interview. It should be positive, clear, and genuine. Confidence should be conveyed by bankers during the opening. Confidence is an abstract quality; bankers' ability to demonstrate it is directly related to their preparation, experience, and familiarity with the opening process. The steps of consultative opening are not designed to substitute for individual style and experience but rather to accelerate developing a style that is effective, professional, and individual.

Summary

Preparation is essential if bankers are to be effective. They should utilize the opening to earn the attention and interest of the customer. During the opening the sales environment is established. Bankers of course must be on time for their appointments if they don't want to spend the interview recouping lost ground or making excuses. If because of travel arrangements they are delayed, telephone calls should be made.

Preparation is essential if positive openings are to be achieved. Preparation includes a planned format for the opening process and the content. The greeting and introduction, summary, ice breaking, selling of the interview, and bridge question provide the framework around which bankers can effectively and confidently introduce their ideas and earn the right to uncover the customer's Motivation Lever.

Motivation Lever

The Key to the Sale

The objective of the Motivation Lever is to identify and understand the customer's needs. *It is the key to the sale,* the most important part of every sales interview, since it is the part in which bankers gains insight into the customer's needs and point of view. During the Motivation Lever the customer is encouraged by questions to reveal his or her needs, interests, or situation.

There are two questions that are pivotal to uncovering the customer's Motivation Lever: the first has to do with the customer's *present situation* or method of doing something; the second aims at *clarifying the degree of satisfaction* (strengths and weaknesses) with the customer's present system. With answers to these questions, bankers can use further questions and product knowledge to highlight alternatives or opportunities. Unless bankers can uncover the customer's Motivation Lever, they will have to guess at what would interest customers and solve their problems or improve their situations.

Just as bankers are responsible for talking in the opening, the customer should be encouraged to express his or her ideas and needs during the Motivation Lever segment of the sale. The Motivation Lever is uncovered when the *customer talks* about his or her problems, concerns, situation, current banking relationships or methods of financial management. After summarizing the events that led to the interview and stating the general objective of the sales call, bankers are in an excellent position to ask the customer if they may pose some questions to determine the possible value or advantages of a product. These bridge questions encourage a customer to express his or her thoughts about particular banking needs or related needs.

The questions should be more worthy of bankers and the customer than simply a general "How's business?" Unless the customer's situation is understood, bankers cannot consult effectively. If, for example, bankers think there may be a need or opportunity for Direct Deposit of Payroll, they would say, "Before discussing some ways that we possibly can increase efficiency and reduce costs in your payroll operations, I would like to find out about your current system. How are you currently doing your payroll?''

By asking questions early in the interview, bankers give their customers the opportunity to express their needs and interests, and bankers in turn can match those needs and interests with their bank's products. The idea of asking for customer input early in the sales call may be foreign to bankers who make monologue presentations, but it is essential if products are to be discussed relative to customer needs. The information revealed during the Motivation Lever provides the basis of the sales dialogue that will follow.

By identifying a customer's Motivation Lever *before* discussing a product, bankers can eliminate the laundry-list syndrome of going through a list of products, or of the feature and benefits of a particular product, trying to hit on something that interests the customers. The Motivation Lever concept keeps the horse before the cart; it enables bankers to identify needs and concerns first and then to suggest products or solutions. Bankers must diagnose before they prescribe! By understanding the customer's Motivation Lever, bankers can also assist the customer in *identifying* and solving their problems.

The Motivation Lever is the hub in the consultative sales approach. It is the element that differentiates consultative selling from high-pressure or door-to-door selling. It is also the segment that, as experience with several thousand calling offices shows, is the most difficult to utilize. Finding a customer's Motivation Lever requires questioning and listening skills. It also requires patience and self-control. It means asking questions and listening for five, ten, fifteen, or more minutes to the customer's reply, and picking up *all of the key concerns* expressed by the customer, then referring to and utilizing the information throughout the sales call.

The Motivation Lever part of the sale is initiated by a bridge question in the opening. It places the ball in the customer's court. Bankers are often reluctant to do this because they fear losing control. Control, however, is achieved by directing the sales interview, not monopolizing it. The Motivation Lever segment helps bankers to understand the customer's orientation and to focus on relevant products and relevant benefits. *Customers buy benefits,* and the Motivation Lever reveals the specific benefits that will be of value to the customer. For example: the fact (feature) that the Stock Transfer System provides a printout in 24 hours may be of no concern to a customer who is having shareholder problems because of complaints about inaccuracies in names, amounts, and so on. But the fact that the bank's stock transfer system is completely on line and verified by a clerk, which results in virtually 100% accuracy, is a benefit that will be of value to the customer. The customer's Motivation Lever in this situation is to reduce shareholder complaints. Bankers who can identify problems are in a good position to solve problems and increase market share. Questions that are asked *early* in the sales interview are the key to unearthing needs and maximizing opportunities.

The best way to develop customer interest is to have the customer talk about his or her plans, problems, needs, and goals. Unless the customer is given an opportunity to talk about a situation, bankers will not be in a position to maximize sales opportunities because they will not recognize them!

Bankers cannot relate their products to customer needs unless the needs are made visible. Needs must be recognized and acknowledged by bankers *and* customers. Too often bankers perceive needs, then attempt to sell without establishing with the customer that the need or benefit exists and is important to the customer. Although some customers are keenly aware of what they want or need, many are not aware of possible savings in time, money, opportunities, or more efficient systems. Bankers should be prepared to help customers recognize needs and opportunities and understand and accept alternatives.

Summary

The Motivation Lever is the central point of consultative selling, and all other elements of the sale revolve around it.

Action step		Opening
Sales environment		Probing questions
	Motivation	
Incremental close	Lever	Constructive listening
Body signals		Features/Benefits
	Objections/Responses	

The purpose of the other nine elements are to develop and satisfy the Motivation Lever. The Motivation Lever makes the other elements work by ensuring that they are relevant to the customer's situation. Identifying the

Motivation Lever enables bankers to individualize their sales calls, to meet the diversified needs of customers, and to consult with their customers in a professional, competent, and action-oriented manner. When the Motivation Lever is identified, meaningful dialogues ensue.

The Motivation Lever is discovered through customer input; and customer input is primarily evoked through probing questions. Most customers will respond to relevant consultative questions. However, bankers should be prepared with backup questions for less responsive customers. After asking questions bankers should be prepared to listen to their customers' replies and use what they hear to connect their customers' ideas and perceptions with their bank's products, services, and capabilities. How well bankers can connect their customers' needs and orientations with the bank's capabilities will determine how successful they will be in consulting with their customers and increasing market share through the sale of noncredit and credit services.

Probing Questions

Defining Probing Questions

One of the most important functions of probing questions during a consultative sales interview is, to identify the customer's Motivation Lever. Probing questions enable bankers to identify the customer's needs and interests. They play an important role in developing a consultative sales interview, since probing questions are the primary tool for developing a dialogue.

Probing questions are open-ended questions that require more than a "yes" or "no" reply from the customer. Close-ended questions (questions that elicit a "yes" or "no" response) should not be used, since they provide little or no information about the customer's needs, motivations, plans, or thoughts and give bankers at best a fifty-fifty (yes-no) chance of further pursuing a particular topic. By using questions that begin with *what, when, where, how, why, to what extent,* and so on, bankers create dialogues and gain valuable insight and information into their customer's thinking. Valuable questions can also begin with phrases such as "How are you presently...?" and "How satisfied are you with...?" "What are your thoughts on..." or "What effect would...have...?" "What specifically...?" "What alternatives are you considering?" "What is included in their offer?'' ''When are you planning...?'' ''Who currently...?'' Such questions give the customer an opportunity to participate in an exchange of ideas and give bankers information they can use to formulate and develop their product discussion relevant to the customer's situation, needs, and interests.

Probing questions constitute a vital part of the consultative sales approach. Early in the sales interview they provide consultative bankers with a way to identify the customer's Motivation Lever and to create customer involvement. Probing questions also enable bankers to clarify objections and to test for agreement and understanding.

Unfortunately, probing questions are perhaps the most underutilized selling tool that bankers have. Without using probing questions, bankers run the risk of making long-drawn-out presentations that do not necessarily address the customer's needs or spark the interest of the customer. Bankers who make monologue presentations often engage in what appear to be high-pressure or canned presentations. Without probing questions, it is very difficult to involve the customer, and without involvement the customer's interest wanes. Including the customer, addressing his or her needs, or individualizing the sales call is almost impossible without probing questions.

Probing Question during the Sales Call

Probing questions are the sales tools that convert the one-sided sales *presentation* to a *sales interview* in which there is an exchange of ideas. Probing questions create a sales dialogue. They should be planned prior to the sales call and can be used to:

1 Establish the customer's willingness to give input and to assist bankers in finding the customer's Motivation Lever: ''First, I'd like to ask some questions, if I may. How are you presently handling your payroll?'' (Payroll Service, Direct Deposit of Payroll)

2 Find out about the customer's present situation or attitudes: ''What thoughts have you given to...?'' or ''How satisfied are you with your current ability to maximize overnight investments or pay down your loan?'' (Balance Reporting)

3 Assist a customer in recognizing and accepting the existence of a problem or an unsatisfactory situation: ''What has been your experience with late deliveries?'' (Import Letter of Credit)

4   Identify specific competitors or preferences: "What alternatives are you considering?" (Balance Reporting)

5   Narrow down a general statement or vague objection such as "My statement is *always* late!" "When was the last time we were late with your statement, so I can look into this and find out what seems to be the problem?"

6   Discuss and compare Total Offers: "What is contained in their offer so we can compare value and pricing?" (i.e., Account Reconcilement)

7   Probe for qualifying criteria: "How many checks do you issue per month?" (Account Reconcilement)

8   Clarify objections: "In what way is your payroll complicated?" or "How specifically do you think you may lose control of your accounts receivable?" (Direct Deposit and Lock Box)

9   Test for understanding or agreement: "How helpful will it be for you to receive your domestic balance information by 9:00 a.m., in time to make investment decisions?" (Balance Reporting)

Probing Questions are multipurpose, since they enable bankers to:

1   Qualify a customer (qualifying criteria).
2   Create customer input and participation (consultative dialogue).
3   Identify customer needs, problems, and satisfactions.
4   Gauge the degree of customer understanding and agreement (incremental close).
5   Create customer awareness by assisting customers in selling themselves by reaching their own conclusions.
6   Modify their discussion to address customer concerns or perspective (flexibility and shifting of gears to address the customer's needs).
7   Determine priority products or features and benefits to be emphasized (key features and benefits of interest to the customer).
8   Increase bankers' control of the sales interview (by using a question to return to a topic).

Probing Question Traps

Bankers reduce the effectiveness of their probing questions when they interfere with the customer's opportunity to reply. Typical kinds of interference include: answering their own questions by hooking their own answers on to the end of the questions, thereby losing the value of the question, offering the customer alternative answers, not giving the customers time to answer completely, turning questions into statements or explanations, or stringing a group of questions together. Customers should be given time to answer and should not be prompted or interrupted. Bankers should use their judgment in determining how much silence time to allow before speaking to fill the void. The danger lies in giving too little time, not too much. Silence can be an effective sales tool for bankers and customers alike, and bankers should learn to withstand and use it to their advantage. As far as using multiple questions, customers and even bankers themselves cannot keep track of two, three, four, or more questions strung together. Since customers usually answer the last question they hear, important questions can get lost in the crowd. Multiple questions can confuse and even threaten customers and do little to increase the banker's information or control. Bankers should ask one question at a time and wait for an answer. Unless bankers ask one question at a time and patiently and attentively listen to the answers, they might as well not ask them.

Presentation versus Interview

When they fail to utilize probing questions, bankers engage in monologue presentations. The alternative to the monologue presentation is a sales interview, in which the customer is given an active role in the selling and bankers are frequently rewarded by being given an active part in making the decision. In a monologue presentation bankers may monopolize the selling portion of the sale, but customers monopolize the decision portion. In a dialogue both bankers and customers are actively involved throughout the sale.

Summary

Probing questions create an environment in which both the bankers and customers participate in information development and decision-making. Questions not only stimulate involvement but also increase the banker's control of the interview. By using open-ended questions to uncover needs, clarify information, redirect discussion, control discussion, and check for understanding and agreement, bankers are in a better position to control not only the sales interview but also the sales results.

When bankers ask questions they must be prepared to listen to the answers. Waiting quietly will encourage customers to respond. Asking probing questions is only part of developing a dialogue; listening to answers is the other part.

Constructive Listening

The Listening Side of Selling

A significant amount of selling takes place when bankers are listening, not talking. Since it is what customers themselves say or think that determines the decision, it is important that customers be given the opportunity to state their ideas. It is only when customers see the value or recognize a need themselves that they are motivated to buy. Customers often sell themselves based on the information that they provide to the bankers concerning their own needs and situation. Bankers can help customers sell themselves by listening to find out what is on their minds and using that information in suggesting solutions, improvements, or alternatives. When bankers do most of the talking, they have no way of estimating whether or not they are on target, whether their ideas are of interest or value to their customers, or whether customers understand and accept their ideas. It is important that bankers give their customers the opportunity to discuss, and that they focus on what is revealed.

Constructive listening is more than simply paying attention to what customers say. In selling, the act of simply hearing is not enough. Constructive listening goes one step further. It consists of first paying attention, and second, constructing or building a response based on what has been stated. Constructive listening is essential if any sales mileage is to be achieved out of the dialogue between customers and bankers. Constructive listening occurs when bankers absorb what their customers say and integrate this information from customers into their own responses. Unless bankers incorporate and utilize what they hear, they might as well not listen.

Constructive listening does not take place as frequently as it should. Bankers often tend not to listen because they think they are two steps ahead of the customer and know what he or she is going to say, or because they are thinking about their own response or, unfortunately, their rebuttal. Sometimes they don't want to listen because they mistakenly think they are relinquishing control by letting the customer speak. Sometimes bankers are so eager to go on with their own ideas that they interrupt their customers. Some bankers don't listen because they think their customers are incorrect in their thinking; but unless they have a specific understanding of the customer's misinformation and misperceptions, they will not be in a position to effect corrections.

Bankers should consciously focus on what the customer is saying even if they find it boring or repetitious, or know that it is incorrect. Although some customers are easier to listen to than others, all customers must be heard if needs are to be satisfied and sales are to be made. Listening does not occur for a host of reasons, many of which are related to ineffective communication skills that are developed in childhood. Good listening skills are, however, invaluable in selling situations, and bankers should work toward developing and improving them. Consultative listening requires concentration, attention, and training. Bankers will be rewarded by an increased number of sales, not only difficult sales but also the "easy" sales that turn out to be "not so easy" because the customer's point of view was not understood and his or her confidence was not won.

Constructive Listening Technique

Bankers can employ constructive listening skills by concentrating on what customers say, storing key ideas (words) in their memory bank, and constructing a mental list. When it is their turn to speak, bankers should integrate the key words or ideas from their list in a positive, supportive way. The word "list" is actually the archaic word for "listen," and the archaic meaning implies remembering and referring to the information that is recorded. The remembering and referring aspects of the word "listen" are essential in a sales situation.

Constructive listening requires that bankers truly appreciate the value of having customers talk. Bankers can start their sales off on the right foot by asking probing questions so that the customer will disclose his or her ideas, concerns, needs, or internal operations. The entire time the customer is talking, bankers should be taking mental notes (sometimes, with permission, written notes) and highlighting in their minds the key words or ideas to which the customer refers. As the customer talks, whether it is for two or twenty minutes, bankers should identify the one or several ideas that are important to the customer and should register and sort them on their mental lists as they are mentioned. After the customer has stopped talking, bankers should use the items from their list to relate their product information to the customer's needs, ideas, or concerns.

Constructive listening has taken place when bankers:

Comment on general items in which they agree with their customers.

Discuss items from their lists and use features and benefits their bank provides as they relate to the items.

Check for agreement and understanding after each item is discussed.

Too often, unfortunately, bankers—and people in general—do just the opposite. When it is their turn to speak, they start off with the way or ways in which they *disagree* with what has been said. Often they begin their ideas with "No" or "I don't agree." Bankers should train themselves to use the customer's point of view by appreciating what the customer has said (recognizing and referring to it) and in a *positive* way tying it with their product advantages or with new information. They should work with their customers, not against them.

Another problem that bankers face occurs when customers present several ideas at one time, and bankers focus on the last point or the point that was of interest to them, rather than focusing on the total picture or total list and covering each idea, one at a time. Bankers must train themselves to listen, to sort out points of agreement and disagreement, to keep track of all the key ideas that they hear, to lead with a point of agreement and support, and to cover all of the points presented. For example, in discussing Export Letters of Credit:

Customer. I'm not too *sure* of the foreign market. We have done *fairly well* with our jeans here and I don't know if we should venture any further. I was in *London* last month and we talked to a bank there, but I'm *not sure.*

Banker. You *certainly* have done *very well* over the past four years, and I can appreciate your *hesitance,* since it would be a new market. May I ask to whom you were speaking in *London*?

Customer. Y Bank, and they went over some procedures with me but I'm *still not sure* it's a good idea. We decided to wait.

Banker.   I think we may be able to help in..., but before discussing
                 some alternatives, may I ask what specific concerns you have
                 about...in doing business abroad?

Customer.   We've done OK here, but we know our customers. My brother
                 and I built this business up. *How do we know we'll get paid?*

By questioning and listening, the banker in the example was able to uncover
the customer's specific concern. The banker developed a selling situation in
which he could address and attempt to satisfy a specific concern in a way
that the banker from the English bank apparently could not. Throughout
the dialogue the banker referred to the key idea expressed by the customer.
By actively listening, the banker showed sensitivity to the customer's concerns, and by listening and probing he was able to narrow down the concern. The banker could then discuss the ways in which his bank could assist
the customer in protecting himself and being assured of payment.

Some techniques to use to develop constructive listening skills are the
following:

Develop a Mental List of Key Ideas as the Customer Talks.   Bankers
should listen for key words or cues from what the customer says. By identifying and utilizing key words, bankers can recognize and pursue opportunities. Following are some examples of the kind of "opportunity
phrases" that bankers may extract from the customer's discussion:

"Causing delays"

"My Treasurer"

"Problems with our subsidiaries"

"Lack of control"

"Turnover"

"X bank has made a proposal"

"Need for more flexibility"

"Our Board"

"Problems with our accountant"

"Have never really thought of you as an international bank"

"Complaints about..."

"We don't have a good handle on our balances."

Phrases like these, as well as many others, should raise red flags in bankers' minds. *Bankers should ask questions to get further clarifications.* The customer's replies may provide bankers with opportunities to solve problems through the bank's credit and noncredit products and services. For instance, the words "we don't have a *good handle* on our *balances*" should be registered and should trigger questions concerning idle balances and reporting systems. When the customer has finished talking, the banker might ask, "How do you presently get your balance information?" "What problems...?" "How helpful would it be to have a consolidated report...to make investment decisions?"

Bankers should cue in to opportunity phrases and pursue them in their responses. Bankers need to pay close attention to any words that are positively or negatively charged in helping construct reasons to buy. General or ambiguous words that customers use can also provide bankers with opportunities. For example, phrases such as "concerned that it's too complicated" or "too time consuming" need to be explored and discussed. When customers use general or ambiguous terms, bankers' questions may help customers narrow down the concern and define specifically what disturbs them. Bankers need to train themselves to *hear* and *use* what the customer discloses.

Draw from the Mental List When Constructing a Reply. The mental list may consist of one idea or multiple ideas, depending on what the customer has said. One idea at a time is more easily handled, since only one idea has to be addressed, but customers often scotchtape several ideas together. When the customer gives several ideas in one response, it is important to respond to the total picture with a general positive, supportive comment and then to address each point, one by one. Use the *customer's words* or at the very least *synonyms* when replying, as a way to tie the product to the customer's needs.

Begin with a Note of Agreement. A comment that acknowledges or supports what the customer has said provides a way to help the customer be receptive and open to communications. Bankers who can develop this skill in sales situations have a great advantage in communicating. The difference may seem subtle, but it is the difference between being positive or negative. For example, in discussing International Cash Letters:

Negative

Customer. But you all use the same airplanes?

Banker. No we don't. We use our own system for scheduling the most timely flights and we...

Customer. We are perfectly happy with X bank and see no reason to jeopardize the relationship for a product that we already have.

Positive

Customer. But you all use the same airplanes?

Banker. It's true that we use the same planes, but because of our attention to flight time and our processing and the availability we provide, we may be able to offer some improvements. May I ask how satisfied you are with the efficiency of the service you now receive? (Or if availability were the competitive edge, the banker could have asked, "What availability do you receive?")

The banker in the positive example used the customer's idea as a building block rather than contradicting or wiping out what · the customer said.

Close Incrementally. Bankers should check for agreement and understanding between themselves and their customers by using probing questions. They should confirm agreement or disagreement *before going on to the next point.* For example: "How might our coordination of flight and processing time assist in reducing...?"

Never Interrupt. Bankers must train themselves to listen and to wait until the customer has finished talking. When bankers and customers engage in "overtalk" during sales calls, the customer always has the right of way. Bankers should train themselves to literally stop talking on a dime when the customer begins to talk in a sales interview.

The following examples contrast a segment of a sale without and with constructive listening.

Snapshot of a Sales Interview without Constructive Listening

Customer. We sell softwear in Japan. We bill our customer in dollars and the amount of the receipts vary considerably. It's hard for us to forecast revenues. It's hard to know what our income is likely to be. We bill in dollars because it is more convenient, since we don't know much about Foreign Exchange.

Banker. We suggest that you hedge your yen exposure in a foreign exchange by using a forward contract.

Customer. Wait a minute. We don't know anything about Foreign Exchange. I don't want to speculate, and I know that my president doesn't want me to speculate.

Banker. I don't think you can call this speculating.

Analysis. The customer's and banker's ideas are clashing. What went wrong? The banker did not refer to the customer's problem but rather rushed the solution, and contradicted the customer.

Snapshot of a Sales Interview with Constructive Listening

Customer. We sell softwear in Japan. We bill our customers in dollars and the amount of receipt varies considerably. It's hard for us to forecast revenues. It's hard to know what our income is likely to be. We bill in dollars because it is convenient, since we don't know much about Foreign Exchange.

Banker. Managing Foreign Exchange exposure does require some expertise. What specific concerns do you have about your invoicing to Japan?

Customer. I want to protect my profits. The way it is working now *we don't know what we'll get for our dollars.*

Banker. *Not knowing what you'll get for the dollars* is a real problem. Would it be helpful if we could work out a way to eliminate the fluctuations and uncertainty of payment and help you lock in what you will be getting and protect your profits?

Customer.   It certainly would.

Banker.   We have a way in which you can be guaranteed a pre-determined rate for your yen, and you wouldn't have to worry about the fluctuations. By using a forward foreign exchange contract, you could be assured of a fixed price so that you would know exactly how much you would be paid. You could base your costs and contracts on that fixed price. You are a dollar-based company, and you need to know easily the amount you are going to get. You can invoice in yen and we can advise you on.... You could set your costs in advance and...profits.... How might that help?

Customer.   It sounds like a good approach, but we don't want to speculate.

Banker.   I can appreciate that you would not want to speculate. By using a forward contract in which..., you would in fact be eliminating risk....

Analysis.   With constructive listening, banker and customer are in sync. The banker constructively listened to what the customer said. He utilized the information in constructing his responses and began to work toward building agreement.

Summary

Dialogue is critical to consultative selling, and listening is one half of the dialogue process. Too often bankers monopolize the sale. There should be an equal-time clause in all sales interviews, to ensure that there is customer and banker *input*. One of the saddest commentaries on a lost sale is: "The customer just did not understand." Bankers have the responsibility to help customers understand how their product will benefit the customer. When the customer does not understand, it is usually because bankers have not listened and thus did not understand which specific aspects confused or concerned the customer. Unless bankers can look at their products through their *customer's eyes*, they will not succeed in satisfying needs and selling the products. The only way to understand customers' points of view is to encourage discussion. Bankers can identify specific concerns by asking probing questions and listening to customers' responses. Unless customers are given the opportunity to discuss their thoughts, bankers will not be in a position to satisfy their needs or concerns.

Features and Benefits

Feature and Benefit Strategy

After the customer's Motivation Lever has been identified, bankers can use the feature-benefit strategy to discuss products or services as they relate to the customer's situation. Although the feature-benefit approach is not new, it remains the most effective way to understand and discuss a product for selling purposes.

It is impossible to understand a product without understanding the features of the product. Features are the traits, attributes, or qualities that the bank puts into the product to make it function. Features basically are the "nuts and bolts" of the product or service. They can, however, when discussed without their corresponding benefits, lack appeal in a selling situation. BENEFITS are the values the customer derives from the product. Benefits point out to the customer how it may be possible to increase profits, reduce clerical expense, and maximize opportunities. Too often, bankers assume that the customer understands the benefits; they think that discussing them would be redundant, unnecessary, pushy, or hard sell. This is an unfortunate assumption, since *customers buy benefits.* Customers usually are not interested in the bank's products for academic reasons but rather for the ways in which the bank's products can meet their needs. Customers are constantly evaluating *what is in a bank's proposition, deal, or product for them.* It is the banker's reponsibility to identify the customer's needs and convey how those needs can be satisfied.

Linking Features and Benefits

Features and benefits should complement one another. By linking features with their benefits, bankers can stimulate interest and help the customer appreciate the product relative to his or her own situation. When bankers discuss the features of the product to the exclusion of benefits, they are in danger of falling into the "nuts and bolts" trap, in which they risk boring their customers with what appears to be information not related to the customer's needs. Linking features and benefits increases bankers' ability to capture the customer's attention, satisfy customer needs, and establish credibility. Benefits are important because customers buy them. Synonyms for a "feature" are trait, characteristic, attribute, detail, aspect, and element; synonyms for "benefit" are value, advantage, and reward. Which have more selling power, features or benefits? Of course benefits do. Benefits, however, are not sufficient; they are incomplete when they are used alone. For benefits to be believed, they must be supported and *linked* to their corresponding features. A benefit cannot exist with a corresponding feature, and one feature may have several benefits. Benefits are the value derived by the customer from the feature. Confidence men make a living selling benefits for which no features exist. Bankers, whose credibility and reputation is of the highest order, can help their customers have *justified confidence* in a product by linking features and benefits.

An example of the feature-benefit strategy for an Import Letter of Credit is:

Feature	Benefits
X Bank substitutes its credit standing for that of its customer.	Increases the customer's ability to do business abroad, since the Letter of Credit assures the supplier of payments.
	Strengthens the customer's ability to negotiate price and terms because of assurance of payment.
	Conserves working capital by eliminating the need to pay cash in advance.
	Broadens the customer's sources of supply.
	Enables customers to meet a supplier's request for payment via Letter of Credit.

Feature-benefit selling enables bankers to *relate* the product to customer needs by demonstrating the *responsiveness* of the product to the customer's situation. Regardless of how on-line, superior, or advanced a product's technology is, it is of little or no interest to customers unless they understand how it will meet their needs or improve their situation. The feature-benefit approach helps bankers communicate value to customers. Many experienced bankers report that there is nothing more useful in talking "product" with customers than the feature-benefit approach.

Each product has a number of features and benefits. Through questioning bankers can identify which specific benefits respond to the customer's Motivation Lever and are apt to spark and sustain customer interest. By addressing key benefits, bankers can avoid reciting a laundry list of features and benefits hoping to hit on the key one(s). Rather than discussing all of the features and benefits of a product, it is essential to home in on those that relate to the customer's needs.

Summary

By taking the time to understand both the features and benefits of a product, by consciously linking them during a sales call, and by focusing on the particular features and benefits that relate to customer needs, bankers can help satisfy customer needs and expand the market share of the bank. Features and benefits are the heart of sales-oriented product knowledge. They should be used to explain, discuss, or describe a product. They enable bankers to relate what the bank puts into a product with what the customer will get out of it!

Objections

Objections as Sales Opportunities

Objections are an integral part of sales interviews. They are a natural and important part of every sales interview. Bankers should welcome objections as a sign of interest and attention from the customer, and use them as an opportunity to explain and clarify. When they are overcome, objections can provide bankers with a way to advance in the sale; when they cannot be fielded successfully, they can save time by helping bankers recognize insurmountable obstacles. If the objection in fact cannot be offset by the product's total offer or product's options, bankers should recognize the barrier and save valuable time. *Objections become negative factors in selling only when they block what should have been viable sales opportunities.*

Customers object for a host of reasons. Some customers may be testing the bankers or challenging their competence; some may be contrary or merely require proof. Some may object because they are apprehensive about making a decision or fear making a wrong decision; others may lack technical knowledge or authority to make the decision and are reluctant to admit it.

Although there are probably as many reasons for customer objections as there are customers, there are essentially two kinds of objections. The first is the genuine objection. Genuine objections are voiced by customers who honestly do not understand the product. If the banker had the same misperceptions or lack of information about the product as this kind of customer, the banker would also object! The second kind of objection is the "role" or "staged" objection. Role objections are used by experienced customers to test the bankers' knowledge and check professionalism or competence. Such customers see as a part of their role as customer the responsibility of going through a scenario, most of which is already well-known. This, they believe, is a way to do the job and to be able to make a decision with confidence. Role objections occur frequently in negotiations in which both seller and customer are required to assume roles. Frequently after a heated but resolved negotiation a customer will say, "You really did a great job," to which the banker will respond in a positive and appreciative way, "You weren't so bad yourself!" Nevertheless, whether objections are genuine or staged, bankers should take objections seriously and work toward overcoming them. Both kinds of objections are an important part of selling.

Regardless of their motivations, customers' objections are valid and must be fielded by bankers if sales opportunities are to be realized. To exploit the positive opportunities in objections, bankers should consider *all* objections as *signals* from the customer for more information or additional clarification. The underlying reason for most customer objections is a *need for more information* concerning the value or benefits of the product. Unless bankers can field objections, they may lose viable opportunities to complete sales or make quailty referrals to specialists.

Product knowledge, linking features with benefits, is of course essential in overcoming objections, but it is not enough. In addition to having the product knowledge necessary to address the objections, bankers should be able to *communicate information* without directly affronting, confronting, contradicting, offending, or frightening the customers. When handled properly, objections can be used as a ladder for making the sale, since each objection can be an opportunity to inform the customer and to build rapport and establish credibility.

Objection Response Model

The way in which an objection is fielded is as important as what is said. The Objection Response Model provides a process for fielding all objections. It is designed to be applied to all objections to help *turn them into positive selling points*. The Objection Response Model is a vehicle through which bankers can effectively communicate their product information. It consists of the following four basic steps:

1 *Repeat the Objection* (echo or restate the objection). Echoing or restating the objection assures the customer that his or her objection is heard and understood. It conveys *empathy* for the customer's irritation or concern and reduces the customer's defensiveness and aggression. By defusing the objection and soothing customer hostility, bankers can prepare customers to hear and accept the bankers' replies. Echoing or restating the objection also provides bankers with a moment to compose their thoughts.

2 *Ask a Clarifying Question When Objection Is Vague.* Very often objections are general. Clarifying or narrowing down an objection makes it more manageable. It is almost impossible to satisfy a vague or general objection. For example, if the customer objects to the bank's Account Reconcilement System by saying, "Those systems have too many problems!", the banker's response should include, "I can appreciate your caution, but *what specific problems are of concern to you?*" By qualifying or narrowing the objection, the banker can address specific concerns and work toward satisfying them. If the customer reveals a concern about lost checks, the bank's new automated system, with a built-in verification mechanism and special check location coding, may satisfy that concern. Another example would be a customer who says, "I did not receive my account analysis" or "My statement is always late." Bankers should respond, "I'm sorry that there seems to be a problem Mr. _____ . Could you tell me the date of _____ so that I could look into this immediately?" By showing concern and narrowing the objections,

bankers are in a better position to satisfy them.

3   *Apply Product Knowledge* (features and benefits relevant to the objection).   Bankers should use their product knowledge to satisfy customer concerns. By linking the features and benefits of the product, bankers can assist the customer in understanding the *value* of the product to him or her. Objections provide bankers with an opportunity to discuss the capabilities of the product and to help the customer appreciate the value that he or she can derive. Bankers should use objections as opportunities to enlighten and inform customers, in a clear and relevant way.

4   *Use the Incremental Close.*   Each time bankers respond to an objection, they should *check* with the customer to find out *if the answer satisfied the concern.* By using open-ended questions to close incrementally, bankers can check for comprehension and agreement before proceeding to another point. The incremental close serves as a barometer for the sales call by checking on the extent to which the customer understands and accepts the bankers' ideas and information. It assists bankers in determining their next step (to proceed in the sale, backtrack, or switch gears). An example of an incremental close is: "How does our ability to trade in all major currencies, including..., satisfy your concern about our versatility?" During the incremental close, it is what the customer, not the banker, says that is important.

Bankers who do not use the Objection Response Model often find themselves in a "yes-no" argument or contest with their customers. By applying the Objection Response Model, bankers can turn objections into positive selling points.

The specific words or phrases that bankers select are a matter of professional and personal style; nothing should be done to interfere with or replace their individuality. On paper the model may appear rigid, but when the words and tone are chosen by bankers to suit their conversational styles, the model becomes invisible. The model is effective in reducing customer resistance and in assisting bankers to communicate their ideas. Unfortunately many bankers attempt to field objections by giving product knowledge without taking the time to repeat and clarify the objection. After they discuss their product and information, they fail to check for understanding and agreement on the customer's part, and therefore are not as effective as they might be. Bankers should experiment with the Objection Response Model in nonbusiness as well as business situations to determine its effectiveness in improving communications and establishing agreement or clarity. The Objection Response Model provides a communication *process* for satisfying objections by understanding and clarifying the objection and testing for understanding and acceptance from the customer.

Of course, before any objection can be resolved, it must be understood. As soon as the customer begins to object, bankers should stop talking. Besides being courteous, this indicates concern for the customer and avoids over-talk, in which both parties are talking at the same time and sheer volume reigns. In a sales interview, when overtalk occurs, the customer has the right of way! By being quiet, bankers can encourage the customer to express his or her concern or criticism. Bankers should listen carefully to the *complete* objection. By giving the customer time to elaborate on the objection, bankers can gain valuable insight into the customer's thinking, which they can then use in formulating their responses.

The four steps of the Objection Response Model provide the foundation for turning objections into sale opportunities. Some experienced bankers say that they can benchmark the progress of the sale by the sequence and handling of objections. The Objection Response Model is designed to provide empathy (repeat objection), clarity (clarifying question), data (product knowledge), and customer feedback (incremental close). It should be used by bankers whenever they face a significant objection.

Bankers should welcome objections as opportunities to look at the product from the customer's point of view. Unless bankers are willing to look at the product from the customer's perspective, they should not be surprised with the customer's reluctance, refusal, or inability to understand the benefits of the product as the banker sees them. The Objection Response Model puts bankers in a better position to establish an *advocate* rather than a neutral or adversary role. As advocates or consultants they can work with the customer toward developing mutually beneficial relationships. Bankers have the best opportunities for success when they understand their customer's point of view before they try to promote their own. Customers are more willing to work with bankers who are trying to solve problems, rather than with bankers who are trying to sell products.

Objections are one of the best ways bankers have of seeing the product or situation as the customer sees it. It is the responsibility of bankers to help the customer appreciate the value of the product, but unless they appreciate the customer's perceptions or misperceptions, they cannot work toward changing them.

The Objection Response Model is designed to improve communications at crucial moments throughout the sale. If bankers cannot overcome, offset, or neutralize objections, they risk losing the opportunity to complete the sale or make a referral to a product specialist. When customers object, they are in a negative mode. As bankers respond to objections, they work toward establishing a positive mode. Unless bankers succeed in restoring a positive environment, sparks will fly, and although bankers may win a point, they may lose the sale or the relationship. It is important that bankers utilize objections as opportunities to sell. Bankers should combine sales-oriented product knowledge (features and benefits) with effective communication skills (Objection Response Model). Regardless of how accurate the product content of the bankers' responses may be, unless it is communicated in a positive way, customers will not fully accept the information, or they will seek an alternative banking source whenever one is available.

The Challenge of Objections

The Objection Response Model is the basic strategy for resolving objections that can threaten a sale. Bankers should be prepared to face the challenge of objections. They should expect the following objections as a sign of a viable sale.

Price Objections

Resistance to Price.   Bankers continuously face the price objection, "Your price is too high!" Price objections are inevitable regardless of price. Customers often say "the price is too high" or "you're too expensive" even before price is discussed.

Bankers should expect and be prepared for price resistance. Price objections are often closing signals from the customer. If they are not fielded properly, or if they are addressed prematurely by bankers, viable opportunities can be lost. Failing to satisfy price objections not only results in loss of sales but also in a loss of morale for bankers.

Price Traps.   When bankers are fielding price objections, they are in the *negotiating* phase of the sale. It is a high-intensity phase that requires control, skill, and preparation if sales opportunities are to be realized. Unless handled properly, bankers faced with price objections can fall into price traps. Bankers fall into price traps when they make excuses for the prices or blame someone else, rather than exploring and addressing the objections and comparing value.

Typical price trap responses are:

Customer. Your price is too high.

Banker. *We have to make a profit too.*

Customer. Your price is too high.

Banker. *You're right, but I'm just told what they are.*

Customer. Your price is too high.

Banker. *My hands are tied. With the cost of money to us, what else can we do?*

Customer. Your price is too high.

Banker. *For a company of your size, this is the figure.*

Customer. Your price is too high.

Banker. *Well, we can lower it.*

Customer. Your price is too high.

Banker. *No it isn't. X bank charges one cent per item more!*

Customer. Your price is too high.

Banker. *I don't have the authority to change it.*

Customer. Your price is too high.

Banker. *So is everyone else's.*

Customer. Your price is too high.

Banker. *We accept balances.*

Customer. Your price is too high.

Banker. *You get what you pay for.*

These responses put the deal in jeopardy. They place the banker in an argumentative, defensive, weak, or at best neutral position. Each response takes the price objection at its face value, rather than understanding the reasoning behind it and comparing alternatives and value. *Each time one of these phrases is uttered by bankers, sales opportunities are in danger* of being lost. Rather than defending the price, transferring the blame to the bank, the marketplace, the customer, or the competition, or rushing to change the price or conditions, bankers should acknowledge the price objection, *explore* it with the customer, and evaluate it to compare total value. Giving the customer the opportunity to explain his or her objection does not amplify it; having a customer explain his or her objection is the first step in satisfying it! An effective way to avoid the price traps is to utilize the *Total Offer Approach*. The Total Offer enables bankers to understand the objection and to discuss it relative to total comparative value to the customer. It often helps customers sell themselves as they answer their own objection.

Total Offer Approach. The Total Offer will help bankers avoid being trapped and defeated by price objections by encouraging the customer to appreciate the cost-benefit ratio. The Total Offer consists of two parts:

1 Finding out what the customer is comparing the product, deal, or service to in considering it too expensive:

"What are you *comparing* it to in considering it too expensive?" (Comparison is the key!)

"In *relation to what* do you consider the cost to be too high?"

2 Making a comparison of the bank's total product, ideal, or service with other alternatives:

"I think if we compare total packages you may find..."

By making a comparison, bankers and customers can evaluate alternatives, cost, and value. To employ the Total Offer, bankers must understand *what their products are being compared to*, so that they can discuss cost relative to value (compare apples with apples, not apples with oranges). Bankers should help customers compare values, and to do this they must uncover details about competitive offers (another bank) or the alternatives (in-house system) the customer is considering. Without the total offer, bankers may find themselves involved in a comparison of unequal offers, in which their price may be justifiably higher because their product is superior in customer value. Often if bankers were to trim off the additional features for deals in which their price is higher, their price would be comparable. This, however, often results in trimming off benefits that are important to the customer. Competitive offers or products can *appear* to be comparable on the surface, but by exploring the specific *features* and *benefits* or *requirements of the competitors* bankers may uncover substantial differences in the value and in the ability of the products to satisfy customer needs.

Although the Total Offer is a technique for responding to all price objections, it is especially valuable in situations in which the bank appears to have a higher price or when the bank's price is in fact higher. By comparing the bank's total offer with the total offer of a competitor, bankers can often demonstrate that although the products *appear* to be the same, the total packages may be significantly different. By pointing out additional features and benefits that are of value to the customer, by examining compensating balances or qualifying criteria, and by comparing the total relative value of products, bankers may show that the price difference represents value differences. The total offer is designed to protect the bank's profit while demonstrating to the customer the value to him or her. The Total Offer (in comparison to what) is the most effective way to field price objections and build mutually profitable long-term relationships.

The Total Offer capitalizes on the fact that price is a major but *not* all-important factor considered by the customer in his or her decision to buy. To keep price in its proper perspective bankers should discuss their total offer (features and benefits, pricing, terms, the banking relationship, the personal service, etc.)—the *entire package*, whenever they discuss price. Bankers should never discuss price until all of the relevant features and benefits of the deal are understood by the customer.

The Total Offer technique also assists bankers in withstanding customer pressure strategies in which customers in an attempt to test bankers, by alluding to nonexistent competitive offers or alternatives. Bankers who ask for specifics concerning the other offer are less susceptible to such pressure strategies. By politely asking customers for specifics, bankers can assist customers in realistically evaluating their alternatives. By using the total offer, bankers can politely test a customer's sincerity and the accuracy of his or her information.

Cushion Approach. To help discuss price, bankers can also use the cushion approach to convey confidence as they state the price. The cushion approach utilizes timing, tone of voice, and key benefits. Bankers often unintentionally convey a lack of confidence in their price by pausing before and after they state the price and by lowering their voices or inflecting the end of the word as they state the price. For example, they might say, "18%" with their voices going up on dollars, followed by a pause in which they seem to be waiting for the boom to be lowered by the customer, as it frequently is.

It may be more effective for bankers to consciously avoid the delay or pause by introducing price with a benefit and immediately following the price with an additional or special benefit that the bankers have been saving—hence cushioning the price. Pricing information must be delivered with confidence, and the cushion approach reduces the hesitation and insecure intonation that often accompanies the delivery of a quote.

Premature Price Objections.   Deals should be understood before price is discussed or before price objections are fielded. With price objections, bankers should first determine if they are advanced enough in the sale to accurately discuss price. Banking products are often complicated because they contain options. Unless bankers understand the *customer's specific requirement* and have determined and fully discussed the features and benefits that will benefit the customer, it is impossible to properly or accurately discuss a price or respond to price objection. Price objections can be fielded successfully only when the value is fully understood by the customer. Customers who say, "Just tell me the price, before anything else," are frequently more than willing to *delay* discussing price, if the delay is justified by the need to find out the customer's specific requirements so that accurate prices can be quoted. Bankers must recognize situations in which more information is required in order to avoid discussing price before the deal is fully developed or understood. A rule of thumb is that price should not be discussed until there is a time investment (allowing for information and interest) on the customer's part.

Pricing is really the negotiations part of the sale. Uncovering needs, explaining the product, and establishing the desire and securing the decision to buy is *selling*. Settling on rate, price, or terms is *negotiating*. Selling sets the tone, readiness, and commitment for the negotiations. When pricing comes up too soon, bankers should use the inquiry about price as an opportunity to gather specific information. This takes some courage at first, but when handled politely and consultatively, bankers can strengthen their position. An example of delaying answering a price objection is: "So that we can address price relative to your requirements, let's look at the specifics: How many employees would be covered?" Or "I'd like to find out a little about your requirements to enable us to discuss price accurately." Or "Fine, let's look at the specifics. What...?"

Although bankers should always be given pricing information on all products, there are times when they should not discuss price, since the price is negotiable based on conditions, options, or the customer relationship itself. In a situation in which price should not be discussed, bankers should use the customer's question or objection about price as a lead-in to setting the appointment with a specialist.

Sometimes bankers are tempted to give ball-park figures. Although this may be necessary, it can be dangerous, since customers tend to hear the low side. One of the best ways to defer discussing price is to state that it is competitive and suggest setting an appointment with a specialist who could discuss price based on the customer's requirements, his credit situation, or the total relationship with the banks.

Price Trauma.   Price is a sensitive issue even when the product involved is of the finest quality and bankers have confidence in the quality and pricing of their products. Even some bankers who have confidence in their bank's products shudder when price is mentioned. *They often assume that any question or mention of price is an objection.* The reason for this "price trauma" stems from a preconditioning by customers or other bankers. Since banking has become such a competitive and volatile industry, bankers are continuously being bombarded with pricing complaints and objections. Bankers should remember that price is one of the many *features* of their products. They should address questions about price as they would about any feature—by linking it to its benefit, and they should use the objection model when price objections occur. They should discuss price by linking the cost with value. Bankers equipped to field price objections in a consultative manner have an advantage in responding to and satisfying the objection because they can assist the customer in appreciating the value to him or her. The objection response model and the total offer will not only assist bankers in selling a product that is competitive but also one that is superior. Too often bankers lose deals even when they have a superior offer because of their inability to help the customer fully appreciate the superiority of the product and the benefits to him or her.

Confidence in Pricing.   In fielding price objections, bankers should have confidence in the value and merit of their product and its ability to assist the customer. If bankers do not believe in their bank's products or pricing policy, they won't be able to maximize selling and cross-selling opportunities. Without confidence and respect for their products and pricing, bankers can be their own worst enemies. Too often bankers believe that their products are not competitive in price or quality. Often the data from which they draw conclusions is hearsay; in many situations competitors' products are *similar*—not identical—in price and quality. There are in fact substantial differences in the capabilities and operations of most banks' products, contrary to the myth that all banks' products are the same; competitor banks are simply unable to ascertain one another's differences. If bankers assume that their products are not competitive, or that the pricing for a product is out of line relative to competitive prices, they should channel this feedback to their managers so that the information can be verified or the misperceptions can be corrected and when necessary the products can be improved. Feedback from bankers can be used to initiate product improvements and verify or correct internal and external perceptions. Misperceptions from the field must be corrected if the sales force is to function in a confident and aggressive way. When perceptions are correct and products are not competitive in price, value, or hardware, banks must correct the situation or face the price they will have to pay in lost opportunities for having noncompetitive products. No amount of product knowledge or consultative selling skills can consistently compensate for a product that is not competitive in price and value or a sales force that does not believe in its product. The bank and bankers alike should take the time and energy to find out about their competitors' products if they are to succeed in the highly competitive market environment.

Competitive Objections

There are two kinds of competitive objections: "the other offer" and "my present bank."

The Other Offer. The "other offer" objection is similar to the price objection, except that the customer objects by referring to a better offer made by a competitor bank. The Objection Response Model and the Total Offer technique should also be used to field all competitive objections. It is *impossible* for bankers to respond to a competitive objection *unless they know the specifics of the other offer* or of the alternatives under consideration. By asking, "Could you tell me a little about their offer so that we can compare service and pricing?" or "You mentioned that X bank has an attractive package; what in particular did you find of interest to you?" or "You mentioned you were speaking to another bank, may I ask . . . ?", bankers can retain control, while helping customers evaluate their options. If the customer is using the competitive objection as a pressure strategy, the total offer assists bankers in testing and withstanding the objection. When the customer states that he or she has a competitive offer or is looking at the competition, *bankers must make an attempt to get the specifics of the offer* or find out as much as possible about the alternatives that the customer is considering so that they can construct their total offer accordingly and also so that they can assist the customer in comparing and evaluating relative value.

To field competitive objections successfully, bankers require up-to-date competitive information. When bank intelligence cannot provide specific competitive information or cannot supplement in-house information, bankers should gather competitive information from another excellent source, their customers. Bankers who ask, "What alternatives are you considering?" or "What's in their deal?" often gather a wealth of useful information that they can use to help their customers compare and evaluate alternatives.

My Present Bank Objections. Today many companies are overbanked, and when bankers approach a prospect they are advised that the prospect's present bank handles everything for him or her. Bankers faced with a "my present bank" objection should be prepared to politely inquire about the specifics of what the other bank is providing. Their rationale for this is to assist the customer in comparing and evaluating his or her present banking situation to determine if there are any possible advantages in utilizing another bank to supplement the present service. For example, if a multinational company is using X Bank's Balance Reporting System, the banker can inquire about the timeliness and quality of the reporting and the kinds of reports provided. By identifying the competitor banker, and by knowing competitive information, the banker can ask questions to point out areas for possible opportunities and improvments. For example:

Customer.   X Bank is our lead bank and they provide our balance reporting.

Banker.   I respect your relationship with them. May I inquire...to determine if there are any possible advantages that we may have that could supplement the information you receive: How do you . . .?

Inherent Objections

Just as every retail salesperson hears the objection of "limited display space," bankers will often hear repeated objections for particular products, pricing, or systems. Bankers can take advantage of the *predictability* of certain objections by anticipating them and being PREPARED to field them. For example, when discussing *Import Letter of Credit* bankers frequently hear:

"We use documentary collections."
"We pay everything by check."
"It involves too much paper work."

A discussion of *Automated Payroll* often includes:

"We would spend *more* time filling out *your* forms."
"I don't want to drive downtown just to drop my payroll."
"I use another service."
"We do it in-house."
"It's too expensive" (price objections are inherent in almost every product).

Objections that frequently accompany an *Account Reconcilement* sales call are:

"We have our own system."
"Account Rec systems have too many errors."
"Our volume isn't large enough."

Other common objections include:

"We'll lose our float." (*Direct Deposit of Payroll*)
"You're not on our list." (*Commercial Paper*)
"Your rate is too high." (*Loan, Commercial, or Personal*)
"My customers will object." (*Pre-Authorized Checks*)
"Danger of unauthorized transfers." (*Wire Transfers*)

By anticipating the objections and preparing their responses *before* the sales call, bankers can use their product knowledge to turn objections into selling points. They should field these objections using their product knowledge and the Objection Response Model. Product knowledge, pre-sales-call homework, and experience assist bankers in anticipating objections and resolving them. The banker's responses can provide customers with the information necessary to reevaluate the objection. Customers can utilize the information to evaluate their own needs and possible advantages. For example:

Product: Account Reconcilement	Objection Response Model
Customer. We have an in-house system.	
Banker. I can appreciate the work involved in organizing an effective system and your not wanting to disturb it without substantial benefits. Could you tell me a	Repeat objection
little about your system so that we can determine what possible advantages there may be in . . .? How do you reconcile your account?	Clarifying question
Customer. We have three clerks. . . .	
Banker. What problems. . .?	
Customer. . . . workload control.	
Banker. We may have a way to alleviate the tedious monthly checking account balancing and reduce clerical and administrative cost. . . control over check disbursement. . . . What are your	Linking features with benefits
thoughts on simplifying the reconcilement by . . .	Incremental close

If bankers allow themselves to be deterred by objections without giving a second effort, they may well lose opportunities in which both the customer and the bank could profit. By being prepared for inherent objections and successfully fielding them, bankers can consult with their customers and increase market share.

Bad Experience Objections

If the customer has had a negative experience with a product, service, bank, or particular banker, he or she may automatically reject the banker's ideas because of that experience. Bankers should get the specifics of the experience and determine the extent to which the situation has been remedied or changed. The "Not True Now" technique is very helpful in situations in which a problem existed in the past but has been corrected. This acknowledges the existence of the problem and addresses the *changes* that have been made to improve the situation.

Bankers should be prepared for these objections and utilize the Objection Response Model and "Not True Now" technique.

Customer.	I wouldn't bank with you!	
Banker.	I'm sorry to hear that. Could you tell me why you feel that way?	Repeat objection and seek clarification
Customer.	Two years ago we came to you....	
Banker.	Your reaction is understandable and I regret that the situation occurred. At that time we... Today our management recognizes.... My specific assignment reflects this and perhaps... What are your thoughts on...?	Not True Now technique Incremental Close

By facing the objection in a consultative manner, bankers are in a position to *acknowledge the particular problem, express concern, discuss the changes,* and *work toward reestablishing credibility and building a relationship.*

What-If Objections

Customers often require reassurance in making decisions and seek answers to "what if" situations as a way to feel more confident. *Case histories* are confidence builders. They enable bankers to document results and add credibility to their proposals. Bankers can be specific or general in utilizing the case history technique. When a specific case history is used, bankers should refer to customers who are respected in the industry and who have given permission to be used as references. References should also parallel the new customer or prospect in type of business, size, and so on. Bankers can also use *general statements* such as "It has been my experience," "Most of our customers find...," or "We have found...." to build confidence. For example, in response to the objection to using a regional bank for Foreign Exchange transactions, bankers can cite a company such as a national chain or a local museum for whom they do spot trades and forward contracts in several major currencies.

Ordeal of Change Objections

When a customer rejects the banker's ideas because he or she is comfortable with the system he or she has been using for years, bankers should use the "what has been your experience" technique. Bankers should find out as much as they can about their customer's present situation or system *before* discussing, comparing, or promoting their bank's product. Unless bankers do this they will lack the basis on which to draw comparisons, make suggestions, or successfully point out benefits. Unless bankers inquire about the customer's present situation, they cannot know enough about the situation to make valid suggestions. It is senseless for bankers to ever suggest that they can do something better, cheaper, or more efficiently, without understanding specifically what it is they will be improving. Consider this discussion of Import Letter of Credit:

Customer.	I simply pay everything by check.	
Banker.	The check is an appropriate means of making payments, especially domestically; *but what has been your experience with operational delays until the check has cleared?*	Repeat objection Seek clarification
Customer.	When we work with new suppliers and some old ones it can cause some delays. For instance, our holiday decorations arrived in January.	
Banker.	A delay like that must have been frustrating. An alternative such as a Letter of Credit might help reduce problems like that, because the seller is assured of prompt payment after	Features and benefits

	shipment. Letters of Credit motivate the supplier to ship goods on time because documents received after the expiration date may not be accepted. Also with a Letter of Credit you would not be risking your money in advance of shipment. How helpful would it be...?	Incremental close
Customer.	I think it might make sense but what...?	

If there were no delay problems, bankers might ask about control over proper shipment, increasing supplier base, or negotiations of terms to find if Import Letter of Credit could benefit the customer. By finding out about the customer's situation, bankers can consult with their customers about alternatives that would benefit both the customer and the bank. Bankers who do not take the time to understand the customer's needs before selling will find themselves "hard selling" rather than consulting with their customers.

Smoke-Screen Objections

Smoke-screen objections are those used by customers to mask their real objections. Unless bankers unearth the hidden objections, they may find themselves responding to shadows rather than the customer's real needs. By using probing questions and asking "why" in a consultative manner, bankers can often bring out the hidden objection, address it, or save valuable time. For example:

Customer. Let me think about it. (classic smoke-screen objection)

Banker. This is an important consideration to your company. What specific areas do you want to consider? Perhaps I can provide some additional information.

Customer. It's not that I need more information; I want to pass it by our corporate treasurer.

Banker. That sounds like a good idea. What do you think your treasurer's response will be? What are your thoughts on my meeting with the two of you (or the treasurer) to...?

By gently asking questions to test the objection, bankers can often secure information relative to the genuine objection which will help them stay in the sale.

Vague Objections

Bankers who are confronted by objections often rush to provide an answer even when the objection is vague or general and simply too broad to resolve. The rush may be fatal! Bankers may indeed provide an answer, but the answer may not be remotely related to the customer's concern.

Before answering a broad objection, it is important to find out the specifics. This not only enables the banker to understand the objection and therefore have a chance at resolving it successfully, but it also gives the customer the opportunity to voice any concerns and thereby be *more* responsive to the banker's reply.

Since it is virtually impossible to satisfy a general objection, bankers must have specfics *before* they respond to it. The "Why" technique is particularly useful here. It can change the course of a discussion from negative to positive. It can open doors and reduce defenses. Using the "Why" technique enables bankers to understand the specifics of the customer's objections and thus grasp what is really bothering the customer. By narrowing down the objection and responding to the customer's explanations, bankers can position themselves on the customer's side rather than on an adversary side. As he explains why, the customer often begins to satisfy or answer his or her own objection or to reveal a further hidden objection. For example:

Customer. Our employees would never accept Direct Deposit.

Banker. I can appreciate your concern for your employees' preferences. But *why* do you think they would resist?

Customer. They have a right to choose their own bank and they don't want us telling them where to bank, and I don't think we should!

Banker. We at X Bank agree with that, and although there are additional benefits to employees who choose us, employees can have their net pay deposited to *any* financial institution in the country that participates in the Automated Clearing House. Our specialists will provide active support in encouraging your employees to accept the plan. How does that address your concerns for your employees' banking choices?

The "Why" technique can even assist bankers in fielding one of the most difficult credit-related objections: "I don't want to give my personal guarantee." By asking why rather than explaining to the customer that it is necessary because of bank policy, or some similar reason, bankers can often get information that they can use in successfully handling the objection.

By asking why, bankers can avoid making *costly assumptions* that may result in lost sales. A well-positioned, consultative "why" is unfortunately one of the most underutilized words in sales. "Why" can make bankers aware of the customer's needs, concerns, and goals, and thus can produce new data that can significantly reshape the deal. "Why" can also be a time saver; if a customer has a substantial reason that cannot be offset by the total offer, bankers can recognize the situation early and save valuable time. Consider this discussion of Direct Deposit Payroll:

Customer.   We can't use Direct Deposit here.

Banker.   Why is that, Mr. Smith?

Customer.   On two given weeks *none* of our paychecks are the same, and we change them up to twelve hours before.

Banker.   (Banker's product knowledge of qualifying criteria tells him that his bank requires two-day lead time.) Then your payroll doesn't lend itself to Direct Deposit. Your payroll sounds rather complicated and perhaps it could be demanding on you and your staff. How do you handle it?

The banker did not belabor Direct Deposit but began to explore Payroll, a new possibility.

Bank Image Objection

Almost all banks are targets for the Bank Image Objection. Objections such as "your earnings, your size (too big or too small), your location, the fact that you are regional or a money center, operations (manual or automated), your management, the article in, a merger, or a . . ." must be responded to by bankers before anything else can be accomplished. When the objection is basically one that is widely recognized such as earnings, bankers should acknowledge the concern and briefly discuss the bank's position. When the situation has or is about to be improved, bankers should document the improvement.

When the objection is more subjective, such as regional versus money center, bankers should capitalize on the strengths of their position and describe the benefits, whether they are personal attention (small) or a vast correspondent network (large), to assist customers in appreciating the particular advantages to them. For all subjective bank image objections there are usually two sides, and bankers should be prepared to accentuate the strength of their position.

With all Bank Image Objections bankers should work toward increasing the customer's confidence in the bank. The best way to achieve this is through a prepared and responsive reply that is brief and nondefensive. Bank Image Objections must be overcome if market penetration is to be increased and perceptions or misperceptions are to be changed.

Turnover Objection

The Turnover Objection, "You are my fourth account officer in the last ten months," is an objection that many bankers face daily. Reorganizations, promotions, retirements, pirating, and career changes result in what seems to be excessive turnover among bankers. This kind of objection is best handled before it occurs. The transition should be made smoothly and professionally by the present account officer or by a manager. Ideally a personal introduction should be made, and when that is not possible, the manager should telephone the customer to discuss the change and promote the capabilities of the new account officer. The new officer should be completely debriefed about the new account(s). When there is excessive ongoing turnover, managers should stress their management overview role to the customer. If turnover is excessive, management should review its reward structure, training, and organizational system to identify possible contributing factors. A stable sales force is very important in effective relationship management.

Insurmountable Objections

Insurmountable objections are just that! In spite of the Objection Response Model, product knowledge or the total offer, some objections *cannot be offset.* When bankers probe, gain an understanding of the nature of the objection, and address it, they sometimes find that the objection cannot be overcome. For example, a customer may require information at 8:30 a.m., and the bank's Balance Reporting may not be able to deliver it until 9:00 a.m.

Bankers should recognize the paramount weight of the particular objection and be prepared to shift gears. If they cannot do so, the interview may be terminated. Not all objections can be overcome. Sometimes the product cannot accommodate a customer's needs; sometimes a customer may be irrational and not open to ideas in spite of advantages. Recognizing insurmountable objections requires judgment. Bankers should respond to insurmountable objections by acknowledging them. Bankers should be the ones to say, "From what we have discussed, it looks as if this may not be the product (deal) for you." This requires courage, but recognizing and facing such objections does in fact save time and can also save face. It can also have the side benefit of uncovering smoke-screen objections or finding new opportunities. In concluding a topic or an interview, bankers should remember the often-repeated saying: *never burn bridges.*

Premature Objections

Sometimes a customer will raise an objection too early in the sales interview for bankers to handle it adequately. Banker must be prepared to recognize this when it happens and subtly request that a particular point be delayed for a few minutes. Evaluating the readiness to discuss a particular objection is a part of controlling the sales call and bankers should remember that they don't have to respond to an objection or question immediately. They can acknowledge the objection and suggest that it be covered a little later. Bankers should of course remember to address the point that was shelved later during the interview. Pacing objections is quite different from attempting to avoid them. Objections must be faced and even *unearthed* by bankers, since objections that are dodged are likely to reappear as major barriers later in the sale.

Manipulative Objections

Although many objections are genuine, bankers should be prepared for objections that are used by customers to *manipulate the situation.* There are a number of pressure objections, such as better offers, other opportunities, threats to pull the account, being overbanked, and others. Pressure objections can be obvious, such as "We'll pull our account," or subtle, such as "I need a decision now because I'm going on vacation." By looking at the total relationship or by asking specifics, bankers can show their concern, gather specific information, and *test the authenticity of the objection.*

The predominant attitude of the pressure strategy objection is "take it or leave it." Bankers should be prepared to test the waters if they don't want to fold under the weight of a ploy. The Objection Response Model is very helpful in withstanding and overcoming pressure objections. Open-ended questions that require the customer to back up, explain, or further define what he or she has said are the best tools that bankers have to counteract a manipulative customer. Bankers should use these tools coupled with their judgment and experience in handling this kind of customer and establishing a working relationship.

Objections Bankers Can't Answer Immediately

There are basically three situations in which bankers should not attempt to answer an objection (or a question):

1 When they don't know the answer.
2 When although they know the answer, the marketing strategy for the product requires that because of the options, complexity, or sliding scale for the pricing, the specialist be called in to discuss technical questions or objections.
3 When bankers are not sure how to position the answer or to what extent to commit the bank and they need time to review the situation or to consult with their managers, specialist, or committee.

If an objection is raised for which bankers do not know the answer, they should *admit* that they do not have the details, state that they will research the information, and of course report back to the customer. Not having a particular answer can often be used by bankers to their advantage, because it creates the perfect opportunity to arrange an appointment for a specialist. However, overreliance on specialists cannot substitute for preparation. To recognize opportunities and to develop them, bankers should know the basics of the products marketed in their area.

When an objection or question is raised that requires input from specialists, bankers should use the objection as an opportunity to gather information for the specialists, so that the joint call can be more fruitful. For the wide range of products that require technical assistance, a joint call *with* the specialists is appropriate. If bankers cannot give specific pricing because the price is negotiable or a study is required, bankers basically should defer the price to the specialists. Price objections on noncredit products, as well as questions that require technical expertise, analysis, or negotiation, should be deferred to the specialists.

An example of making a referral to the specialists for Direct Deposit Payroll is:

Customer. I think we'll lose our float.

Banker. That's an important consideration. When do your employees cash their checks?

Customer. Within a few days—some three or four days.

Banker. In companies like yours, we have found that the reduction in check processing costs...usually more than offsets the reduction in float. What are your thoughts on having me arrange an appointment with Tim Jones, our cash management specialist, who can review your specific situation and give you some projections....

Customer. Fine, I'd like to really look at what it will mean to us.

Banker. Let's set the appointment for later this week. Would Thursday morning...? Also it would be helpful if I could get some preliminary information so Tim can prepare for the call. You have 500 employees; from whom can I get...?

Bankers can also delay answering an objection in situations in which they are not prepared to commit themselves. They can say that they'd like to take a certain subject back and review the options, give it more thought, or confer with colleagues. For example, in discussing Foreign Exchange:

Customer. Can't I use my present line?

Banker. That is a good question. However, to ensure that you have use of that line for your..., we will open a Foreign Exchange line for you.

Customer. For how much? Can you give me X dollars?

Banker. I'd like to take this back and meet with our credit committee to ensure that we extend to you the maximum line that reflects our relationship with you. I'll be in touch with you on. . . .

Deferring answering an objection to another meeting or a later date can be a helpful sales strategy. Deferring objections is totally different from avoiding objections.

In the long run objections cannot be avoided or circumvented, since they are likely to reappear and block the sale at a later time. But deferring objections can give bankers the opportunity to plan a strategy that will satisfy the customer and protect the interests of the bank.

Customers Who Don't Object

Objections can take many forms. They can be blatant criticisms and complaints; they can come in the form of questions; they can be delivered sarcastically or humorously; they can be spoken without a word, with a raise of an eyebrow, a tilt of the head, or a rub of the nose indicating rejection or annoyance. But what does it mean when no objections are raised? A sales interview without objections often signals trouble. It can indicate boredom, disinterest, or even courtesy. Objections at the very least reflect customer attention and appraisal. They also provide bankers with valuable insight into the customer's thinking.

Bankers should *welcome* objections as opportunities to sell the merits of their products relative to customer needs. They are so important that bankers should ferret them out. When objections are not forthcoming, bankers should test the customer by asking some questions aimed at uncovering concerns and reservations. If a customer does not raise an objection that experience says should be asked, bankers should use questions to stimulate the objections and encourage the customer to express his or her reservations.

Particularly if bankers think there is an objection that could block the sale at a later time, they should raise the point in a nonthreatening manner. For example, in selling a Trust Service, it may be appropriate for bankers to ask, "What are your thoughts on having your *attorney* join us for our next meeting?" Since the attorney may be a key figure later, bankers can gain information concerning the attorney's role, and create the opportunity to develop a relationship with the attorney. Objections that will be stumbling blocks later should be raised by the banker as a way to propel the sale forward. Unearthing and exploring important objections does not increase problems, but rather prevents them.

Summary of Fielding Objections

The key elements of a sale are employed in fielding an objection. Bankers actually orchestrate minisales each time they respond to an objection. The opening (repeating the objection), probing questions (clarifying the objection), Motivation Lever (identifying the customer's concerns), product knowledge (total offer of features linked with benefits to satisfy the objection), and the incremental close (checking for agreement) are all utilized in satisfying objections. Perhaps the secrets to fielding objections are: to allow for customer input; to refrain from giving product information until customers have had an opportunity to disclose what is on their minds and what they really want and need to know to make a decision with confidence; and to respond in a positive rather than contradictory manner.

Bankers should use the Objection Response Model to communicate their product information. By developing the dialogue as they answer objections, bankers are in a better position to make certain that they are responding to and *satisfying* what is on the customer's mind. Customers who are encouraged to express their concerns and who are asked for their feedback concerning their satisfaction with banker's replies are often more receptive to accepting new or unfamiliar information.

It is not usually the inherent *differences* among products or systems that cause a customer to choose one banker over another, but it is bankers' ability to *communicate* the differences or *explain* the similarities relative to the customer's situation that distinguishes one bank, one product, or one banker from another. Product knowledge of course is essential if bankers are to overcome objections, but product knowledge alone is not enough. Bankers may have a great deal of product knowledge, but unless they can consultatively communicate it, they may be unable to convert customer resistance into customer confidence with the information that they provide. Objections must be answered in a way that keeps communications open so that bankers and their ideas can keep coming back. Product knowledge combined with the Objection Response Model increases bankers' ability to convert objections into selling points and helps them advance in the sale.

Incremental Close

Checking for Understanding and Agreement

Unlike a traditional closing in which the banker asks for the order at the end of a *sales presentation*, the incremental close, a periodic checking for understanding and agreement, should be used *throughout* the *sales interview*. By using probing questions incrementally to determine if the customer agrees with and accepts the information that is presented, bankers can gain insight into the customer's reactions, evaluate their own effectiveness, and determine the appropriate next step.

Incremental closing should be used throughout the sales call. Unlike the traditional close that occurs at the conclusion of the sales presentation, or the trial close that begins midway, the incremental close is used during every important part of the sale as a way to benchmark progress. Checking for acceptance every time an important point is covered can eliminate the painful sting that many bankers associate with the traditional close, since they will have an indication of the customer's decision based on his or her step-by-step feedback.

Bankers can nail down points of agreement and address obstacles *as they surface*, rather than let them accumulate until the end of the sale. By involving the customer throughout the sale, bankers are less likely to be surprised at the end of the interview since they would have achieved closure on the major points discussed. Incremental closing also enables bankers to flexibly adjust their approach to the customer based on his or her direct feedback. Bankers can also use the incremental close to guide and pace the discussion and prevent unproductive and unwarranted jumps from topic to topic without ever achieving closure.

The incremental close assists bankers in building agreement, identifying points of disagreement, determining their positions, focusing on customer concerns, and helping them *predict* the customer's readiness to buy. Using the information provided by the customer, bankers can estimate the appropriateness of asking for the order. Incremental closing creates an environment in which bankers can be in sync with their customers, and the final arrangements are not so much the close but rather the *action step* in a *series of agreements* or incremental closings.

Using Probing Questions

Probing questions are the basic tools of the incremental close; incremental summaries can also be used in conjunction with probing questions, but since it is what the customer says that is most important, probing questions should be used as the primary tool for closing incrementally. By using probing questions to test for understanding and agreement throughout the interview, bankers are able to appraise their progress, to confirm points of agreement, and clarify points of disagreement so that they can move forward in the sale. The customer's responses will reveal areas of discord and harmony and will help bankers determine whether to proceed ahead, backtrack, probe, or redirect the sales interview. By asking such open-ended questions as, "How would...contribute to your pool of management information?" or "What are your thoughts on this?," bankers can better estimate their effectiveness *during* the sales call and make the necessary adjustments to respond to the customer's thoughts and needs. Also by summarizing briefly during the interview, bankers can advance in the sale and increase the likelihood that the customer is with them and that they are with their customers. Many bankers state that they would like to be able to "read" their customers. Although body language is extremely important, the incremental close provides a direct and objective way to understand what is going on in the customer's mind relative to the sales call. By using probing questions to close incrementally, bankers can build an ongoing feedback system into their sales interviews.

Reducing Rejection

Bankers who do not close incrementally may find themselves without the order at the end of the sales call, not knowing what went wrong. Reluctance to utilize the incremental close often stems from a desire to avoid negative feedback. Unfortunately, ostrich thinking results in wasted time and wasted effort and does not alter the negative responses that the customer may have. On the contrary, being aware of a customer's negative thoughts can provide bankers with the opportunity to recoup the sale. Bankers should be prepared to test the waters so that they can evaluate their selling effectiveness, identify customer disinterest or concern, make strategy decisions, flexibly adjust their strategy to meet customer needs, and determine the customer's readiness to move into the action step. There is no better way to do this than by using the incremental close.

In practice, the incremental close should be used by bankers as a way to avoid being refused or rejected when they ask for the order. Too often bankers ask for the order before the customer is sold or before the customer has confidence in the value of the product to him or her. Sometimes bankers rush asking for the order because they do not have the product information or the selling skills to sustain the discussion. Some bankers engage in a lengthy monologue description and then ask for the order. This is also risky, since they have no way of knowing how the customer is responding. When faced with a rejection they usually do not know where they lost their customers and therefore cannot reconstruct the parts of the sale that were ineffective. By using the incremental close to check for understanding and agreement throughout the sales interview, bankers can reduce the situations in which the customer rejects the action step.

When an incremental close meets with a negative response from a customer, bankers are at least aware that there is dissatisfaction, misunderstanding, or a lack of interest in a particular area, feature, or benefit. They can probe, reexplain, redirect, or introduce new information. The incremental close does not come with a 100% guarantee, but it does increase the bankers' ability to predict the customer's responsiveness based on the direct feedback provided by the customer.

To meet the competitive pressures in the banking industry, bankers are being told to "ask for the order." Unfortunately, they often ask for the order before the product's features and benefits are understood by the customer relative to his or her needs and interests. Although there is nothing wrong with asking for the order, it is more important to *get* the order.

When feedback from the incremental close is overwhelmingly negative, bankers should *not* ask for the order. The banker should be the one who says, "This does not look like the product or deal for you." This may seem radical or suicidal, but if indeed the product is not right for the customer and he or she recognizes it, bankers can demonstrate their professional judgement, maintain control of the sales call, and save time by also recognizing the inevitable. *When consulting with their customers, it should be the banker who suggests that a product may not be appropriate for the customer before the customer does.* Feedback from the incremental close will enable the banker to do this. Used this way the incremental close can save valuable time, save face, and in many instances assist bankers in saving sales that appear to be lost, by unearthing hidden objections or hidden agendas and reopening the discussion based on new issues or information.

Bankers always need to apply common sense and judgment in estimating the customer's readiness and responsiveness to buy. In the face of customer resistance, bankers should try to satisfy the resistance *before* they try to close. Closing incrementally can help the banker increase sales by checking throughout the sale for the customer's acceptance, rather than waiting until the end of the sale when a *number* of negatives, questions, or concerns may have been built up in the customer's mind, blocking the sale. The incremental close keeps bankers in touch with customer reactions and increases their sensitivity to points of their deals that have to be modified or offset. They also assist bankers in tallying up their areas of strength and deciding when to go for their Action Step.

Some examples of incremental closings are:

General. What are your thoughts on this? How does that sound?

Specific. What are your thoughts on reducing clerical costs and freeing up your staff? How might our automatic tracing help with the problem of uncollected funds?

Summary

The incremental close helps bankers estimate the extent to which they have succeeded in communicating their product's value relative to the customer's needs. It alerts them to the next appropriate step: whether to continue, review a particular area, probe, conclude the interview, proceed in the sale, or implement the action step.

There are six major benefits of the incremental close:

1 It improves communication between bankers and customers.
2 It increases the likelihood that bankers and customers are in sync and stay that way throughout the sale.
3 It increases bankers' *flexibility* in adjusting their sales approach, product emphasis, content, and pacing.
4 It provides bankers with a position of strength from which they can initiate appropriate action steps.
5 It unearths problems, concerns, and misunderstandings and provides an opportunity to correct them.

6 It reduces the number of refusals when an action step is suggested.

The Action Step

The First Step of Implementation

The objective of the incremental close is to lead to a positive *action step*. The action step is the final phase of the incremental close and the first step in implementing the sale. The action step is a natural outgrowth of positive incremental closings. It can be initiated by the banker or by the customer. Often when bankers properly exercise the incremental close, *it is the customer* who initiates the action step by asking, "How do I get started?" If the customer does not initiate the action step, bankers should summarize key benefits and suggest the first step of the implementation. For example: "When would it be convenient to meet with our cash management specialists to discuss your specific requirements so that you can have timely access to your international balances and reduce idle balances?"

Determining Action Steps

Depending on the complexity of the product, the procedures and internal systems, or the size of the bank, the action step for a particular product can include securing a financial statement or other pertinent data, making an appointment with a specialist who will complete the sale, or completing the sale (by finalizing arrangements and signing necessary documents, beginning the implementation of the product, and proceeding with installation).

Since action steps differ from product to product, bankers should have a clear understanding of the appropriate action step for each product and should plan possible action steps before each sales call. For example, if a banker's objective may be to qualify and interest the prospect, gather data such as a schedule of receivables, and to set an appointment for the international specialists.

In initiating the action step bankers should be alert to closing signals from the customers, such as: comments concerning cost, requests for specific information, requests for start-up time, alertness in facial expression, and body language. Closing signals should not be ignored or they can cost the sale. As they initiate the action step, bankers should summarize key features and benefits and points of agreement. The "assumptive close," assuming a decision has been reached, or the "fatal alternative," giving the customer two positive choices, can be helpful in initiating an action step. For example: "Would Tuesday or Wednesday be more convenient?" or "Would you prefer green checks or grey?"

To facilitate decisions and accelerate implementation, bankers should conclude every sales call with an action step. The action step is designed to reduce the number of "hello calls." Action steps should define the *next step*. They should be specific as to concluding arrangements, time and purpose, and participants of the next appointment or next step. *The action step should not be left in the customer's control* or in the customer's court. Bankers must take the responsibility for setting the time, place, and participants of the next meeting *before concluding the interview*. In situations in which a bank specialist or other bank colleagues must be involved, bankers should assume the responsibility of getting back to the customer and making the final arrangements. Whenever possible bankers should participate in the meeting with the specialists and customers.

Contradictory Messages

When customers, contrary to their own positive responses during the incremental closings, reject the action step, bankers should try to uncover the reason for the apparent discrepancy. Unless the customer was insincere in responding positively to the incremental closing, bankers should have anticipated the customer's negative response and should not have initiated the action step. Either the customer was insincere in his or her feedback, or the bankers did not use the incremental close as effectively as he or she might have. As much for their own development as to recoup the sale, bankers should politely ask the customer why it seemed that he or she had agreed with X, Y, and Z, then had decided against the product. This can reveal information that can reopen the sale. If the sale cannot be recouped at the time, bankers should conclude the meeting in a positive and professional manner, always leaving the door open. Whenever possible, bankers should not conclude the interview unless they are satisfied that the objections have been unearthed and discussed and the *total offer* has been presented, reviewed, and understood, even if it is not accepted.

Summary

The incremental close and the action step work together. The incremental close is the traffic light of the sale, indicating to bankers when to stop, when to pause, and when to move ahead. It provides bankers with a way to get direct customer feedback throughout the sales call and signals to bankers when action steps are appropriate. Positive incremental closings usually lead to positive action steps. The action step is the first step in completing, implementing, or installing the product or service. It sets implementation in motion and accelerates bringing in new business.

Body Signals

Nonverbal Messages

The body silently speaks with every gesture. Crossing or uncrossing of legs, the raising of an eyebrow, folding or unfolding of arms, putting on or removing glasses—all these are ways in which a customer unintentionally and genuinely communicates his or her reactions or thoughts.

Customers continuously send out a stream of body signals, both positive and negative. Bankers who are sensitive and alert to body signals are in an excellent position to use the nonverbal cues to their advantage. Before looking at some specific body signals that can be revealed in a selling situation, it is important to recognize that there is no universal translation for body signals. Individual differences, cultural differences, and circumstances can influence body language, and bankers should exercise caution in interpreting it, if they are to avoid making generalizations and assumptions that can be costly. Although there is no universal translation for body language, certain gestures do in practice consistently convey particular messages. The following signals and interpretations are examples of gestures that occur frequently during sales interviews.

Body Signals	Possible Sales Implications
Clasped hands behind head, elbows out	The meeting is over, for all intents and purposes
Putting glasses on	The interesting part has begun
Removing glasses	Disagreement (don't see eye to eye)

Leaning forward	Interested and involved
Backing away	Retreating, touched a sore point
Eye contact	Attention
Arms folded across chest tightly	Guarded negative, threatened, rejecting
Rubbing of nose	Mild or strong *negative* reaction
Tapping	Impatience, nervousness
Doodling	Not interested and wants the topic to be more relevant to his or her needs
Breaking eye contact and quickly glancing down	Listener wants to talk
Closing book, closing pen, moving materials	Overstay of welcome
Hands joined, fingers touching in steeple fashion	Superior, pontificating (I am accomplished and expert in this area)
Legs crossed in toward salesperson	Positive rapport
Legs crossed away from salesperson	Something is wrong and there may be a need to change approach
Pushing chair away from banker	Negative and backing away from the deal
Moving chair in toward banker	Interested, involved, and positive
Customer's choice of chair	Open, supportive (right angle) or adversial, combative (directly across)

These are a few of the many body gestures that are exhibited during the sales interview. All people, of course, utilize body language as a natural and what appears to be an instinctive part of their communication systems. By reading and using body language, bankers can increase their understanding of their customers and therefore increase their sales effectiveness.

The first step in understanding body language is to consciously register what is being signaled. Once bankers become alert that a body signal has been transmitted, they are in a position to decide what response, if any, to make.

Bankers should be cautious as they ascribe a meaning to particular body signals and should keep in mind that a particular gesture may in fact be signaling a negative or positive reaction of the customer toward the banker, or that it may be a coincidence and have nothing to do with the sales interview or the banker. Bankers can confirm the message by gently asking a question, restating the concern, or finessing a comment to observe the customer's reaction. If it appears that the gesture signaled a negative reaction, bankers should tread gently and make the necessary adjustments to regain ground and to make the customer more comfortable. Bankers who are trying to achieve agreement should modify their type of questions or the point of view or perspective being developed as a way to build or reestablish rapport. The objective of the modification is not to manipulate the customer but rather to reopen the channels of communications.

Bankers should be aware that body signals occur constantly during the sales interview. They are communicated through facial expression, body gestures, glances, and posture. They can accompany verbal language or can be spoken silently when no sound is heard. Body signals often start communicating before a single word is emitted.

By taking the time to observe them and make the necessary adjustment to capitalize on positive signals and to initiate a different approach to minimize or eliminate the negative ones, bankers can increase their effectiveness.

The following is an example of using a body signal during a sales interview to *supplement verbal messages:*

Situation	Body Signal	Possible Sales Implication	Banker's Response	Result
Banker is seated in customer's conversation area. Banker is on chair and customer is on sofa at a right angle. Banker makes a comment or asks a question and customer crosses leg away from banker and rubs nose.	Crossing leg away from banker and rubbing nose.	May signal that customer is becoming defensive. Generally these are negative signals.	Banker should soften or rephrase what he or she said, ask a nonthreatening question (one the customer can positively answer), or give a supportive comment.	Customer's defensiveness should be reduced; legs will probably be uncrossed, or cross in toward the banker.

Of course, body signals should be evaluated in conjunction with verbal messages. Sometimes they support the verbal message and sometimes they contradict it. Bankers should use their judgment in choosing which message to respond to. Missing body signals can be as much of a problem as misreading them, and bankers should apply both judgment and experience in reading signals to use them to their advantage.

Summary

Since body signals can give insight into what interests, bores, pleases, or threatens customers, they are important in sales. They should be used with the other key elements, especially the incremental close which provides direct verbal feedback to communicate more effectively with customers. As important as the customer's body signals are to the bankers, the bankers' body signals are often more important. The whole concept of first impression relates to body signals. The manner of entering an office gives clues to attitude, confidence, experience, and rank. Bankers should be conscious of their own body signals and should communicate attention and interest in their eye contact and body posture. Understanding body signals requires alertness, observation, and sensitivity—three qualities necessary in consulting with customers. Body signals should be used to supplement the verbal messages communicated by the customer.

The Sales Environment

The Setting for the Sale

The sales environment—the place and time in which the sales interview is held—is a peripheral but important element of the sale. Because of the nature of the seller-customer relationship, it is usually the banker who initiates the call and who travels to the customer's office or site. Some facilities that are provided by customers are conducive to a sales interview, and some are less than ideal. In a private and comfortable setting, bankers can more easily get the attention of the customer; the challenge becomes much greater in offices or sites that are hotbeds of activity filled with interruptions, telephone calls, stoppers-by, and all the other factors that disrupt and interfere with the sales interview.

Since bankers are the ones who are calling, they usually have little control over the kind of setting they will find. There are, however, certain things that they can do to control the environment they are given, so that they can maximize the time they spend with their customers. The following aspects of the environment effect the call and can have a positive influence on the sales call when they are understood.

The Office

Bankers can take sales cues from the environment, particularly the customer's office. Offices are designed in a variety of ways. They may be bare, crowded with pictures, disorganized, functional, or elegant. Many customers have the bare essentials—a desk arrangement and perhaps a separate conversation area—and some have elaborate settings. Regardless of the kind of office, bankers should keep their eyes open and observe and utilize it to their advantage.

Bankers should be alert to the setup of the office. The office itself can provide the topic for breaking the ice, and if it is the customer's own office (beware: it might not be) it can give insight into the customer's interest or approach. An example is the case of the customer with a book on expensive foreign cars on his desk. The customer spoke enthusiastically about his new car with the banker for about ten minutes. Later in the call when the banker discussed the stock transfer system, he tied in "finest quality" and "image to the stockholders" in a positive and constructive way. An office often reveals something about the customer that the banker can use to understand the customer and satisfy his or her requirements.

No Office

For many middle-market bankers or bankers who visit on-site, customer offices or at least private offices with closed doors are a rare luxury. Bankers often find themselves meeting with their customers standing up amid an active business environment. This situation is most difficult, and on the whole consultative selling cannot consistently take place in such an environment.

Identifying needs and discussing products require the attention and focus of the banker and the customer. Trying to conduct a sales interview amid interruptions and distractions can be disturbing and unsettling, and usually proves unproductive. There is no solution to this problem except to use the active environment to gather basic information, ask some probing questions, identifying possible needs, show concern, and set a time to meet when there is less activity—after five, before nine-thirty, a luncheon, a dinner, an invitation to the bank to see a particular operations area, or a luncheon at the bank. In general bankers (in a sales role) should visit the customer because it is usually more convenient for the customer. In situations in which the customer's environment repeatedly proves to be distracting to the sales interview, it is advisable to remove the customer from the environment or to reset an appointment to a time that is more convenient and less distracting for the customer and the bankers.

Office Seating

Most often bankers are offered a seat *across* the desk from the customer. This is perfectly acceptable and should be graciously accepted. Although it is the most common office arrangement, it is the least desirable for the seller. It presents several significant sales problems. First, the desk can be a barrier separating the banker from the customer; second, a subordination role can be implied; and third, it establishes a "lock horns" or adversary position. Bankers cannot do anything to change the seating arrangement short of moving furniture, which is of course (usually) unacceptable. One top negotiator, when given a lock-horns opposite seat, moves it an inch or two as he sits down to throw off the adversary arrangement, unless it is his aim to lock horns. Similarly, a photo recently printed in *The New York Times* showed two world leaders with their backs to the camera, moving heavy arm chairs to create an advocate right-angle arrangement and eliminate the lock-horns seating arrangement.

So too bankers should be conscious of the seating arrangement and should attempt to use it to their benefit. Some customers have a choice of chairs near their desks. Bankers should wait for a signal from the customer indicating where to sit, but should move toward the *right-angle* seating whenever it is an option. Right-angle seating is conducive to consultative sales since it represents an advocate relationship. When there is a seating arrangement around a coffee table, bankers should also try to avoid a lock-horns arrangement. They must think quickly and select seats that will complement (not oppose) the place in which their customer is sitting or is apt to sit.

Continuous Interruptions

When there is a continuous stream of interruptions—telephone calls, questions, problem solving, miniconsultations, stoppers-by—it is virtually impossible to consult with the customer. During a sales call plagued with interruptions, bankers should be patient and understanding and should not show annoyance or indignation or take the confusion or possible rudeness personally. The customer expects the banker to be sympathetic to how busy he or she is. If the interruptions do not stop, bankers should supportively acknowledge the busy schedule and *suggest that a new time be set that would be more convenient for the customer and more conducive to discussing the customer's situation, requirements, and opportunities.* Bankers should use their present appointment as an opportunity to set the next interview, perhaps to be held at a restaurant or at the bank or during off-business hours.

Time

In a broad definition, the time allocated for the meeting is also a part of the selling environment. Bankers should have an idea of the amount of time that they will have with the customer and should prepare accordingly. If the time that had been set for the meeting is cut short, bankers should resist the temptation to try to fit one hour's worth of discussion into fifteen minutes. When meetings are shortened bankers should gather some preliminary information and use their time to interest the customer in the next full interview.

As for the best time to have meetings, morning hours before lunch are generally optimal times; however, bankers should avoid the "not a good time syndrome" that puts off meetings because it's Monday, Friday, after lunch, too late in the day, too early, near a holiday, and so on. Although judgement must be used in scheduling sales time, and some days (such as July 3 if it falls on a Monday) may not be the best time, all business and many non-business hours are prime time for selling.

Summary

In looking at the relationship among the ten elements of a sale, the environment is a peripheral element. It is the setting or frame in which the consultative process takes place. Bankers have less direct control on the environment than any of the other elements, since it is usually on the customer's home court. The environment, however, is an important factor. Bankers can't reconstruct the environment they are given, but they can *look* at it and make decisions about how they can use it to maximize their valuable selling time and support the consultative tone of their sales call.

Summary of the Ten Elements of a Sale

By understanding the ten elements of a sale, bankers can prepare for and conduct productive sales calls on a more consistent basis. Many bankers are seeking ways to maximize the time they spend with their customers. They are seeking assistance in making more effective sales calls. The sales call is really the manifestation of the precall planning. A major factor in the success of a sales call is the *preparation* of the ten elements. Bankers should prepare for each element prior to making a call. Whether the call is a prospect (first) sales call, or a sales call with an established customer, bankers should flexibly utilize the ten elements to achieve their sales objective. Whether the objective of the call is general, such as establishing rapport, identifying needs, learning about the customer's situation and recognizing possible opportunities for the bank, or more targeted, such as establishing a need for international services and introducing the bank's international capabilities, the ten elements should be used.

The ten elements should be a part of all sales calls with prospects and customers alike. Of course the nature of the relationship will influence the depth of each element. Prospect calls will focus primarily on establishing rapport and identifying needs through the opening, Motivation Lever, and probing questions. However, unless objections are fielded successfully, incremental closings are applied periodically, and appropriate features and benefits are discussed, there may not be a second call. And unless an action step (the next step) is determined, the call may become another "hello call" with minimal potential for new business. So too calls with established customers must utilize all of the ten elements, with the appropriate emphasis on each element.

Although sales calls with existing customers are often more focused in their objective, and based on their knowledge of the customer and previous calls bankers have preselected a product or product family to explore, they should avoid falling into the trap of introducing the product without first establishing need and interest (Motivation Lever) on the part of the customer. When assumed needs do not exist, bankers should be prepared to switch gears. Probing questions will help establish genuine needs.

Using the ten elements during *all* sales calls will assist bankers in achieving their objectives. The time frame, pacing, and sequence of the elements will of course vary according to each customer and customer relationship, but the elements should be a constant factor in all sales interviews if consultative sales is to be achieved. It is through the preparation of the ten elements that bankers can *control* the sales call. The customers are the variables, and the ten elements of a sale are the constants. Bankers should approach each sale as professionals who know what they are doing. Of course they should be prepared to jockey the elements to meet the customer's style, but they should not lose track or control of where they are in the sale. The banker's skill in using the ten elements provide a way to maximize control.

The ten elements of the sale provide a basic awareness and approach to sales. They provide bankers with a plan and a process so that the sales interview, although it is *flexible* and *responsive* to the situation, is not accidental or free-flowing to the extent that bankers are just drifting through it, not really sure of their sales objective or sales target. Although bankers should be flexible in the sales call, their flexibility should be based on preparation and choice rather than "whatever happens."

The ten elements are designed to improve communications by creating a dialogue between bankers and their customer. The *opening* is used by bankers to prepare the customer for the interview. The only element that may be dominated by bankers is the opening. The other elements are controlled by bankers but shared with the customer. The Motivation Lever provides bankers with the opportunity to learn from the customer how he or she sees a particular topic, product, or his or her own situation. Bankers should mentally scan during the Motivation Lever part of the sale to find areas of dissatisfaction or areas for improvement. Unless they can pick up and utilize the customer's Motivation Lever, they will miss opportunities to assist the customer and at the same time increase market share. Bankers should use *probing questions* to uncover needs and to stimulate customer input and involvement. They should employ *constructive listening techniques* in understanding and responding to the customer's ideas and needs. Product knowledge of course is the heart of the sales interview, and the *feature and benefit approach* assists bankers in relating the product to the customer's needs. The *Objection Response Model* should be used to clarify, inform, and establish agreement, and the *incremental close* ensures that customers do not become lost or disinterested in a monologue in which they have little or no part. The *action step* puts the sale into motion and converts hello calls into sales calls. *Body signals* supplement verbal information and assist bankers in gauging the customer's responsiveness. An awareness of the selling *environment* helps bankers maximize selling time and maximize the setting for the sale.

Bankers' sales calls should be standardized in that they should use the ten elements as a flexible blueprint for each sale. The ten key elements provide a process *not* a script. They are an invisible vehicle for communicating information in an individualized and complete way. The ten elements are helpful in developing a consultative sales environment. They provide a transferable system that bankers can use to discuss any product or deal. Although products, custoemrs and bankers are different, the underlying sales-communication process for a consultative interview is always the same.

It is very often the bankers' delivery that distinguishes one bank or one product from another, and bankers who utilize the consultative selling approach can orchestrate effective and successful sales interviews with a wide range of customers. The ten elements are important in effective consultative sales calls. With the exception of the opening, Motivation Lever, and action step, the sequence of the elements is completely irrelevant. Bankers must juggle the elements to help the customer sell him or herself. Consultative selling is almost "selling without selling," since the focus of the sale is the customer's needs and not the sale of a product. Many bankers, and others in sales, expect selling to be a tug of war between buyer and seller. The tug-of-war approach to sales is an approach that is devoid of Motivation Levers and a meaningful sales dialogue. The consultative approach to sales works particularly well for bankers because their aim is to develop long-term, mutually beneficial relationships between customers and the bank, which are based on trust and satisfaction. The ten elements are the tools for building such relationships.

PREPARING FOR THE SALES CALL

Preparation is a major factor in the making of effective sales calls and in maximizing sales opportunities. Whether it is a sales call on a prospective customer or a current customer, bankers are required to do their homework if they want to maximize their sales results.

As bankers plan for their sales calls, they should focus on:

1 Understanding the products that are to be marketed in their area.

2 Developing accurate customer knowledge and identifying customer needs.

3 Developing sales plans *before* each sales interview.

Outline of the Sales Call

Prior to making the actual sales call, bankers should outline their sales objectives and activities. The outline of the sales call (written or mental) is designed to help bankers maintain control during the sales interview by avoiding surprises. Outlining the sales call also enables bankers to build *flexibility* into the sales plan.

The outline should include:

Background on the customer.

Objective of the sales call

The approach to open the call.

Probing questions to qualify the customer.

Probing questions to identify needs or problems (product opportunities) and to create an awareness of needs.

Banker's own strengths and weaknesses and customer's assumed strengths and weaknesses.

Knowledge of products that seems appropriate for the customer, at least tentatively.

Tentative priority of features and benefits to be discussed.

Representative customer in similar industry.

Anticipated objections and responses.

Competitive information.

Possible action steps.

Many bankers state that they need assistance with their sales presentation but not with the planning for their sales calls. Much of what takes place during the sale should be deja vu for the bankers. They should have prepared their opening, organized their questions, anticipated the objections, and made speculations based on research as to the customer's possible Motivation Levers. The sales call should be new, fresh, spontaneous, and organized from the customer's perspective, but the essential elements of it *should not be new to bankers*. The sales call should be a reflection of the flexible plan they developed prior to the call. Effective selling is the result of effective preparation and planning. Bankers should be prepared for their part of the sales call and should orchestrate the call to make it a productive use of time for both parties.

Although bankers genuinely separate planning from what takes place during the sales call, it is the failure to recognize the direct relationship between planning for the call and what happens during the call that is at the root of their expressed dissatisfaction with their sales presentations. The observation and analysis of more than one thousand sales calls has made it evident that many bankers expect the call to develop by virtue of the fact that banker and customer are together. In discussing planning, many bankers express their belief that "you have to wait until you meet with the customer." This is at best one quarter true, and it dangerously borders on the "fly by the seat of your pants" school. Certainly the customer's needs, situation, and intentions are key factors in determining what is finally accomplished in the sales call, but that does *not* negate the need to be thoroughly prepared with the ten elements for several possible sales discussions before entering the customer's office. The onus is on the banker to set the stage and guide the sales program. If the customer has a strong grip on his or her needs, options, and plans, the banker's orchestration becomes less difficult, but bankers should never relinquish their responsibilities in hopes that the customer is prepared!

Exhibit 2 is a planner that can be adapted by bankers in preparing for their sales calls.

Exhibit 2 Sample Sales Call Planner

Company: _____   Banker: _____
Address: _____   Relationship: _____
Key Contact: _____   Possible Products to be Discussed:
Date of Sales Call: _____   _____
Kind of Call (prospect,   _____
   nurturing): _____   Background: _____
Purpose of call: _____   _____

Banker's Strengths and Weaknesses	Customer's Assumed Strengths and Weaknesses

Exhibit 2   Sample Sales Call Planner (continued)

Bankers Objective(s)

Customer's Assumed Motivation Lever

Strategy for Opening the Interview

Qualifying Criteria

Probing Questions

Product Knowledge

Features	Benefits		Anticipated Objections	Objection Responses

Sales Environment and Materials

Action Step

Comments

SALES WITH TWO OR MORE CUSTOMERS

Multiple Customers

Frequently bankers are required to meet with two or more customers at the same time. When this occurs it is usually necessary to modify the ten elements of a sale, since sales meetings with group of customers have additional factors that must be taken into consideration. Whether bankers are to meet with a small group consisting of two or three customers (treasurer, cash manager, and foreign currency manager to discuss a cash management system), or a larger group consisting of eight or more (a board of directors to discuss Investment Management or the employees of a corporation to discuss Direct Depository Payroll), bankers should recognize that group sales calls require special preparation and attention if they are to be effective.

Group sales meetings can be more demanding than one-on-one sales calls. With multiple customers, there are usually multiple Motivation Levers. To compound the situation, there frequently is less opportunity to identify respond to, and address each customer's particular need. The dialogue that is the basis of consultative selling on one-on-one sales interview usually cannot be developed in a large group meeting. To compensate for the increased number of customers and the lack of opportunity for one-on-one exchanges, bankers should approach the ten elements of the sale from a slightly different perspective when the group exeeds 10 or so customers. The ten elements should be a part of a sales presentation to a group but with certain modifications. The following factors should be taken into consideration in modifying the consultative approach.

Multiple Motivation Levers

Since individuals in the group often have different objectives and may have conflicting hidden agendas, bankers should be prepared to recognize and satisfy multiple needs and interests.

A Monologue Format

Because of the increase in the number of customers, there is considerably less opportunity to exchange ideas, identify needs, and actively involve participants during the sales meeting. When the number of customers exceeds 10 or so, a consultative *sales interview* (dialogue) becomes difficult, and a consultative *sales presentation* (monologue) may be substituted.

Group Presentation Skills

Communicating with several customers at one time requires an understanding of group communication skills, since each customer expects attention, eye contact, and so on. Regardless of who the decision-maker is, bankers should be cognizant of the group and should establish eye contact and give attention and handouts to *all* group members, whether they be family members, subordinates, operations people, or other managers but also remember to pay appropriate attention to the decision maker.

Sales Environment

The meeting place and positioning of participants should be considered in preparing for the presentation, since it can have an effect on sales results.

From Dialogue to Monologue

The most significant difference between a one-on-one sales call and a sales call with a group is the shift from a dialogue to a predominantly monologue format. During a one-on-one sales call, bankers develop a sales interview with customers. In sales calls with a group, bankers are usually required to make presentations. The degree of direct and ongoing interaction distinguishes sales *interviews* from sales *presentations*. The difference, however, does not preclude involvement and interest. Creating and maintaining the involvement and interest of the participants is more challenging in group presentations, since the greater the departure from a dialogue, the more difficult it becomes to capture and keep the attention of the group. Bankers should compensate for the lack of active, ongoing dialogue by taking additional steps in preparing for the meeting and by building an *adaptation* of the ten elements into their presentations. Although presentations to a group are generally more difficult, they do provide bankers with one advantage. Generally the topic of the meeting is decided on prior to the meeting, and bankers are afforded the opportunity to prepare in detail for the predetermined topic.

Preparing for a Group Sales Presentation

Preparation for a sales presentation to a group gains additional importance, since there is often minimal opportunity to develop responses from the customers during the meeting itself. Bankers should research the composition of the audience so that they can be aware of the various orientations and objectives of the members of the group. Before beginning the sales meeting bankers should identify key decision-makers as well as the key individuals who will influence the decision. Unless they know their audience, they may approach issues or topics in ways that can threaten, bore, or alienate key individuals in the group if not the entire group.

Yellow Pad Technique

The most effective way to prepare for a group meeting is for bankers to conduct *individual interviews* with key customers who will be involved in the meeting or at least with the key decision-makers *prior* to the group meeting. These individual meetings are referred to as "yellow pad" meetings because they give bankers the opportunity to informally take note of each of the customer's needs, interests, and concerns. The notes can be taken mentally or can be recorded, if customer approval is given. Bankers can utilize the yellow-pad data in preparing for their group presentation. These yellow-pad meetings are sometimes thought of as politicking, and in a sense they are. However, it is foolhardy for bankers to meet with a group with little or no idea of the group's modus operandi, orientation, or network. Although they are time consuming, bankers should take every opportunity to arrange yellow-pad meetings with key individuals if they are interested in maximizing the results of the group meeting.

Yellow-pad meetings not only provide insight into the needs and structure of the individuals in the group but also are instrumental in marshaling support and identifying and reducing obstacles. Such meetings help bankers understand the lay of the land. They are a way for bankers to develop rapport prior to the meeting and to reduce the number of surprises or limit the number and magnitude of unexpected problems that may occur during the group meeting. Of course the yellow-pad meetings must be conducted on a one-on-one basis or their purpose is defeated, since individuals often are less defensive and more open when they are approached alone. Yellow-pad meetings are the first step in gaining and maintaining control of the group meeting.

When yellow-pad meetings are not possible because of distances, schedules, internal politics, or other factors, bankers should be aware that they may be entering a lion's den. At a very minimum they should use their liaison in the group to find out as much as they can about each of the group members: who will be there, what their roles are, their history with the company, their backgrounds, their relationships with other participants, and their orientation toward the subject to be discussed.

In a consultative way, bankers should gather as much information as they can. A wealth of information, such as irregularities or conflicts of interests, strengths and weaknesses, can be revealed when questions are asked in advance. In questioning the positions of the participants that would be attending the meeting, a banker found out that one of the participants was not an in-house person but rather one of his competitors! Another banker discovered that one of the participants of his meeting was the individual who designed the system that the banker wanted to replace. In the former case, the banker was afforded the opportunity to tactfully eliminate the competitor from the audience, and in the latter case to modify his criticism of the present system.

Before meeting with any group, whether it be a few individuals or twenty, bankers should have the following information:

What is the objective of the meeting?

What is the topic?

Are the participants aware of the objective and topic?

Who will attend the meeting?

What is the decision-making process?

Who are the decision-makers? (Who has the decision-making authority and who can influence the decision?)

What is the background and orientation of each participant?

What are the Motivation Levers of members of the group?

Is the group a mixture of decision-makers and users?

Will a colleague from the bank accompany the banker?

What is the physical setting of the meeting place?

Where and when will the meeting be held?

How will the banker use the setting?

Where will the banker sit? Stand?

How much time has been allocated for the meeting?

What materials are needed?

When will questions be asked?

All of the above questions are important in developing the presentation. Unless the orientation of the group is understood, bankers could slant their presentation in a way that reduces its effectiveness. As they prepare for a meeting with several customers they should consider seating arrangements and also the appropriateness of making a joint call.

Seating

The seating arrangements are important in establishing an advocate role. Bankers should strive to sit among a group of twelve to fourteen rather than sit at the head of the table or stand apart from the group. Experienced negotiators who are seeking agreement often utilize right-angle or middle-of-the-table seating to develop a positive supportive environment, rather than choosing the head of the table. In selecting their seats around a round, oval, or rectangular table, bankers should avoid positioning themselves head-on with the decision-maker(s) and should aim for right angle (non-opposing) seating. Experienced negotiators or salespeople who are already seated in the meeting room while the participants are arriving, will whenever possible actually change the seat they initially selected, if the decision-maker selects an opposing seat. Rising to get coffee, or to speak to someone can often provide an opportunity to improve one's seating position.

Tandem Selling (Joint Call)

In a sales presentation to a group, bankers are often outnumbered by their customers. Some bankers find it helpful to have a colleague accompany them to help balance the odds or to add specific expertise. This tandem selling or joint call strategy can be effective, provided that the two bankers understand and accept their roles, the sales approach, and the makeup of the group. Their efforts should be coordinated, if they are to avoid working against one another or contradicting one another. Also in a joint call bankers should be cognizant of their seating and should carefully avoid a seating arrangement that suggests "us" against "them" by integrating the seating when they have the option. Also being across from one another rather than next to one another enables bankers to discreetly send messages.

Developing the Presentation

Based on the data they can gather, bankers should prepare for their presentation. As the group exceeds several participants, dialogue selling is usually inappropriate. Although because a dialogue cannot be developed, bankers should not compromise their effectiveness by making a one-sided, long, boring speech. Bankers should *adapt* the ten elements to ensure that their presentation involves the participants and stimulates a decision to buy.

Adapting the Ten Elements

By utilizing the ten elements in a modified fashion, bankers can ensure participation and maximum involvement.

Opening

The opening, as in a one-on-one sales call, is important. Bankers should consider:

How and by whom will the banker be introduced?

Who will summarize the last meeting or the events that led to the current meeting?

To what extent has the group been properly prepared for the meeting?

How will the banker communicate the objective of the meeting so that it is understood and accepted by the members of the group?

How will the banker gain the attention of individuals with different interests?

Clarifying the objective and gaining the interest of the members of the group are essential if sales calls with a group are to succeed. Feedback and evaluations from hundreds of individuals who participated in meetings indicated that they did not know the specific objective of a large number of the meetings they attended before the meeting, and that their speakers did not clearly define the objectives to the group. A five-second statement of the objective is not sufficient, nor is merely stating the topic. Too often assumptions concerning the purpose of the meeting are made, and the assumptions lead to a breakdown in communications.

Too often bankers assume that the participants know exactly why they are there. If internal communications were not clear, bankers may have the full responsibility of explaining the background and preparing the group for the sales call. Bankers should take *several minutes* to define the objective and to sell the idea that the objective is of value to the group before beginning to discuss the topic or product. In group as well as one-on-one sales calls, bankers should find and hit Motivation Levers before they begin to sell. For example, a banker making a presentation to a Board of Directors concerning an International Balance Reporting System might state:

. . . This morning I would like to discuss a possible way to *reduce idle balances* and put those balances to work by investing them in multinational money market instruments. As you know, unless you can identify the funds that are available in time for you to use the information, you cannot maximize short-term investment opportunities. Before I discuss how our bank's Balance Reporting System may. . . . I would like to review the present method. . . as I understand it. . . . or Before I discuss how . . . could you tell me what you see as your . . . so that I can talk about the specifics of our . . .	Stating objective in terms that interest the customer Tying it to an assumed Motivation Lever Restating objective and hinting at benefits Benefits Summary and building comparison (using research in a positive manner) Giving customers opportunity to articulate their needs (motivation Lever)

Features and Benefits

Bankers should link features and benefits and should focus on the feature and benefit that relates to the assumed Motivation Levers if they are to keep the interest of the group. Since participants may not have the opportunity to ask questions concerning benefits that will accrue to them, bankers should spell out the benefits.

Objection and Response

Since customers in a group may not have the time, opportunity, or inclination to raise objections, bankers should anticipate the objections that are likely to be raised in the minds of the participants. By building objections and responses into their presentations, bankers can reduce customer resistance. For example, "Some of you may be concerned about the other bank's willingness to provide us with the balance information...."

Probing Questions

To maximize involvement, it is preferable that members of the group be free to ask questions throughout the sales call; however, when larger numbers are present, this can be difficult, and it is often necessary to suggest a question-and-answer period toward the conclusion of the sales presentation. Bankers should leave ample time for the question-and-answer period and *announce at the beginning* of their presentation how questions will be handled. In addition to using questions from the group to explain the product, bankers can also include rhetorical or thought-provoking questions in their presentations in order to explain, clarify, and stimulate involvement. An example of such a question would be: "How many dollars are sitting idly because data cannot be gathered in a timely fashion allowing for investment decisions to be made?"

Constructive Listening

Although there is not that much opportunity to listen to the customers during the group presentation itself, the yellow-pad meetings should have provided bankers with information they can use in constructing their presentation. With the information gathered prior to the group meeting, bankers can incorporate interests, phrases, and ideas that are relevant to the group. Particular attention should be paid to questions that are asked during the presentation or during the question-and-answer period, since they provide bankers with the opportunity to satisfy customer concerns. After answering *the question, bankers should remember to check with the participant that in fact his or her question was satisfactorily answered.* For example, a question as simple as "does that answer your concern (or question)?" can ensure that the question was adequately covered, and it signals to the group that the next issue can be raised.

Incremental Close and Incremental Summary

Bankers can use incremental summaries, to supplement the incremental close to develop understanding and agreement as they proceed through their presentation. Since participants may not be familiar with the context, there is a danger that they may become confused or distracted. Incremental summaries serve to keep them alert and informed. Bankers should also use a final summary before initiating the Action Step.

Action Step

Just as in a one-on-one sales call, bankers should aim for getting the order. They should plan the desired action step prior to making the presentation. The action step is usually initiated by the banker but can be initiated by one of the participants, usually the decision-maker. If there is a question-and-answer period at the end of the presentation, bankers should complete that period *before* initiating the action step. The reason for this is to establish as much clarity as possible among participants, before seeking commitment to the product or service.

Body Signals

Reading and responding to body signals is much more difficult in group presentations, since they are multiplied by the number of participants. The bankers' own body signals are also important, and maintaining eye contact with the group rather than focusing on the key decision-makers(s) or reading notes. With a group it is important to be enthusiastic without being overly animated in hand or body gestures. (See pages 97–100 for a discussion of Body Signals.)

Sales Environment

The size of the group often influences the selection of the sales environment. Bankers should find out the kind of facility that will be used and the kind of seating arrangements that will be available. When given the choice, bankers should avoid the lock-horns position (sitting directly across from one another), particularly with the decision-maker. They should also position themselves as a part of the group rather than apart from it, for example, by sitting with the Board during the presentation (unless using or writing on a flip chart) rather than standing apart.

Summary

Sales presentations to a group can be demanding, but they can also be rewarding. Preparation through yellow-pad meetings and planning are important if sales results are to be achieved. The ten elements essential in a one-on-one sales call also apply in group sales situations, except that they require some modification to compensate for the increase in numbers. Exhibit 3 is an action planner that can be used by bankers in planning sales presentations to groups.

Exhibit 3   Sales Planner for Presentation to a Group

Product: _____

Banker's Objective: _____

Customers' Assumed Motivation Levers: _____

Time: _____	Decision Maker(s) _____
Date: _____	Number of Customers _____
	Customers' Roles _____
	Environment_____

Opening

Key features and benefits

       Features   *Benefits*

Anticipated objections and responses

       Objections   *Responses*

Exhibit 3   Sales Planner for Presentation to a Group (continued)

Incremental Summaries and Points at Which Summaries Will Occur

Questions and Answers (Q and A throughout presentation or in a Q and A period)

   Anticipated Questions   Responses

Final Summary

Action Step

Materials

Practice, Critique and Modifications

(After completing work sheet, banker should construct a presentation *outline* that can be referred to, not read, during the sales presentation.)

HIGH AND WIDE SELLING

Depth Selling

"High and wide" is a sales strategy that refers to maximizing selling opportunities by earning the confidence and support of *both* the *economic decision-maker(s)* and the *user decision-maker(s)* of a company. The economic decision-maker is usually the high-level contact who has control of the purse strings, and the user decision-maker is frequently a key person in the technical or operational staff who has substantial influence on the economic decision-maker's views because of his or her operational knowledge and responsibilities.

From High to Wide

Bankers frequently meet with the Vice President of Finance (high); unless the bankers also arrange to meet with individuals such as the comptroller or cash manager (wide) and satisfy their needs and concerns, the sale can be *undone internally* by staff members who may undermine the proposal because they were not involved in the decision and feel ignored, threatened, or confused.

Since senior people often rely heavily on operational staff for input, when marketing a product that will affect an internal system or require internal changes, bankers should involve and win over the technical staff. Since managers might not think of involving the key operational staff, it may be prudent for bankers to inquire if it would be appropriate to meet with key operations people. These "wide" meetings can be very helpful, since they enable bankers to gather information as well as marshal support.

For example, in discussing a new Account Reconcilement System bankers may ask, "What are your thoughts on my meeting with your cash manager to discuss...?" or "When we meet with our specialists, are there any members of your staff that you would like to have at the meeting?" or "Would you" "Shall I stop by and introduce myself and...?" Very often the technical person can provide the data that are needed to establish a cost-benefit ratio, and will also be active in the installation of the product. By developing a relationship with a user decision-maker as well as the economic decision-maker, bankers can develop multilevel penetration in the company that will be helpful in advancing their ideas.

From Wide to High

So too if the bankers' initial contact is from the operational (wide) end every effort should be made to meet with senior (high) management. This meeting can be between management and the banker alone, or with the wide contact, the high contact, and the banker. It is always preferable to arrange a direct meeting with high persons or high *and* wide, but sometimes for internal or political reasons, wide persons may choose to act as the intermediary for the bankers. To protect the rapport and relationship established, bankers often must accept this. Whenever possible, they should diplomatically prepare materials that their contact can use or work with their contact in preparing for the presentation. In situations in which it is essential that bankers meet with high personnel and they are unable to get past wide ones, soliciting the support and involvement of a senior officer from the bank [Executive Vice President (EVP) or Senior Vice President (SVP)] for a joint call often automatically elevates the level of penetration without ruffling feathers.

Summary

The important element in high and wide selling is to recognize situations that require depth selling. Bankers should utilize one contact in the company to meet with other appropriate contacts. *Anytime high persons make references to checking with wide or vice versa, bankers should inquire about the possibility of arranging a meeting with the new contact so that they can tell their own story.* It is also very helpful to gingerly question the present contact about the attitudes and background of the new contact *prior* to meeting with him or her.

"High and wide" selling is an excellent strategy for building long-term relationships. Changes in management and promotions are also good reasons for utilizing high and wide selling, to ensure that a relationship does not become seriously weakened because of one change in personnel.

SALES MATERIALS

Professional and attractive sales brochures, exhibits, visuals, and sales aids can be used to increase the communication between bankers and their customers. They can be used during the sales call to imprint key points on the customer's mind, to illustrate complicated points, or to provide customers with examples of the content and format of reports. They also can be used as leave-behind pieces that can reinforce a particular idea after the sales call has been completed.

Sales Brochures

Brochures are a reflection on the bank; therefore they should be professional and attractive. Divisions of the bank should coordinate their customer-directed materials so that they convey a unified bank-wide image rather than a series of unrelated images.

Just as bankers should evaluate the appearance of sales brochures in determining whether or not to use them, they should also evaluate the content. The content of the brochures should reflect a consultative sales approach. Too often sales materials focus exclusively on the operations and features of the product from the bank's point of view without addressing benefits or value to the customer for whom they have been written. By addressing the bank's needs, features, and accomplishments, they fail to provide customers with information relevant to their needs. Unless brochures include in-house capabilities of the products (features) along with the value of the product to the customer (benefits), *they will not generate customer interest.* Unfortunately, because many brochures focus on features or benefits to the bank instead of benefits to the customer, they are relegated to the waste basket. If customers are expected to utilize and refer to leave-behind pieces after the sales call or respond positively to them during the sales call, they should be pertinent to customers' needs and situations. Bankers should use brochures that reflect customers' points of view to clarify and reinforce their products, and should not waste their time with materials that lack such customer orientation.

Sales Aids

Sales aids (flip charts, slides, charts, etc.) are materials designed to be used during a sales call to assist bankers in communicating with their customers. Generally bankers are reluctant to use sales aids, since they seem reminiscent of door-to-door or canned selling. This attitude is unfortunate, because they can be used in an individualized and consultative way and can be of particular value in selling environments in which there are a wide range of products. They are most effective when they incorporate customer feedback through probing questions. For example, in showing a plan for the acceleration of cash flow through a Lock Box, bankers should ask, "How would this improved availability of funds assist your company in meeting its daily cash needs?" Bankers should use the customer's comments to pinpoint and relate benefits in terms of dollars, time, and convenience. Sales aids can be used for basic products and also for sophisticated products. A multinational netting system, for example, can be explained much more simply with a diagram than with words alone.

Sales aids, exhibits, and visuals can help customers understand and appreciate the features and benefits of a product. By showing examples of reports and the kind of information provided, customers can get a hands-on experience with the product.

Other Sales Aids

In addition to brochures and sales aids, there are several special sales materials that can be of significant value to bankers when they are used properly. The are: the written agenda, the specification summary, and the bank's annual or quarterly report.

Written Agendas

Written agendas which outline the objective and content of the meeting can be very helpful to bankers during their sales calls. Agendas are *not* appropriate for all sales calls, however. *They are appropriate only for sales calls in which both bankers and customers are in expressed agreement about the topic or specific product to be discussed.* For sales calls in which the topic has been agreed upon in advance, agendas can increase bankers' ability to lead an organized and professional sales call. Agendas can be used effectively in one-on-one sales calls, but are particularly helpful in a presentation to a small group. Agendas are also very helpful when selling ideas in-house to managers or staff. Almost no important in-house meeting should be held without a written agenda. The agenda assists bankers in developing their ideas and also assists customers in following those ideas.

The agenda should contain:

1 Company, bank, or department name.
2 Date.
3 Objective of meeting.
4 "Agenda" (title).
5 Listing of agenda items.
6 Summary (The last item should be summary.)

Agendas should be distributed *after* the opening and after the customer has had the opportunity to review the status of or his or her thoughts on the topic(s). When distributing the agenda, bankers should say, *"I have taken the liberty of developing an agenda based on our discussion. . . "* As soon as agendas are distributed, bankers should *review* the objective, and briefly review each item to be discussed. Items that are known to be of interest to the customer or suggested by the customer that relate to the objective of the call should have been incorporated into the agenda. Bankers should ask for agreement or suggestions for modification of the agenda items. After securing agreements or adjusting the agenda (adjustments should usually be in keeping with the objective of the sales call), bankers should begin the discussion. With one customer or with a small group, bankers should create a dialogue and accept questions throughout the discussion. For larger groups a question-and-answer period at the end is advised.

Specification Summaries

Specification summaries, worksheets which outline the information needed to implement a product, are excellent selling and cross-selling aids. A specification summary should be developed for each product that *requires analysis by a specialist or technical support from the* operations area. During the sales interview or immediately before or after the action step, bankers can use specification summaries to gather data to be provided to the specialists, or to operations. The information from the specification summary should be used to outline the customer's requirements and to communicate the implementation instructions to operations.

Specification summaries can also be given to specialists to help them prepare for a joint call with the banker. When used for referral purposes they should be forwarded by bankers to the specialists.

Specification summaries should include the following information.

1 Corporate information:
   Name _____
   Address _____   Phone _____
   Decision-maker _____
   Operational contact _____
   Type of business _____
2 Product information:
   Product _____
   Relevant data for each product (i.e., for Direct Deposit: number of employees, frequency of deposit, data input, delivery location or Foreign Exchange: currencies, amount of foreign-exchange activity

($), and suggested Foreign Exchange line)
Options _____
Customer requirements _____
3 Operations interface between bank and customer:
Banker (account officer) _____
Bank specialists _____
Customer contact _____
Implementation date _____
Special instructions _____

A standardized specification summary should not be used for all products, since the product information category for each product will vary and the specification summary should outline the specific data required for each product. The specification summary can be an effective and formal referral document to the specialist when a specialist is required or to the operation area to implement the product.

The Annual or Quarterly Report

The bank's annual report can be an excellent leave-behind piece. It is particularly useful when bankers are calling in locations that may not be familiar with the bank or when discussing products such as Commercial Paper or other investment instruments. Bankers should distribute annual reports as they plan to utilize them or at the conclusion of the meeting, so that customers are not distracted by them.

Distribution of All Handouts

Bankers should selectively choose handouts that they will use and should consciously control the distribution. Unless bankers decide beforehand when and how materials will be distributed and used, they may find themselves in competition with their own handouts for the customer's attention. When distributing handouts, bankers should:

1 Distribute handouts *as they are to be used* (not prematurely in the sales interview), or the customer's attention may become focused on the handout as the banker is talking.

2 Introduce and explain what the handout is and why it is being distributed.

3 For a larger group, state method and time of distribution.

4 Don't waste too much time distributing materials.

Summary

To get maximum effect with all sales materials, bankers should:

1 Be thoroughly familiar with any materials to be used to ensure that they are pertinent and accurate.

2 Put materials *in the order* in which they will be used.

3 Customize materials whenever possible (company's name, date of meeting, clipping on of business card in advance).

4 Maintain control over printed material by distributing it *as it will be used*, not before, since it will distract the customer's attention from the sales interview.

5 Leave appropriate materials behind or send them as a follow-up.

Sales materials can be excellent reinforcement tools. They can highlight or document particular points and can assist bankers in explaining their ideas. They should be used to support bankers in their sales effort but never to replace them or to substitute for a sales interview.

Sales materials can complement the consultative banking approach when they are written from the customer's point of view. Effective sales materials can increase the customer's understanding of a product and serve as a reminder of potential value, improvement, or opportunity to him or her when they are used by bankers in an individualized and timely fashion.

4

Aspects of Developing and Managing Relationships

As a part of their responsibilities, bankers are required to provide their customers with information and assistance on not only their credit needs but also their non-credit and credit-related requirements. They are also expected to develop new business opportunities and to protect and increase present relationships.

Bankers have become total relationships managers. As the liaison between the customer and the bank, they must engage in planning, selling, and follow-up on an on-going basis. An important part of their job is initiating business and prospecting is the first step in developing new business.

Bankers as relationship managers are involved in long-term management. As the cycle progresses from prospecting to nurturing, prospects become customers and customers become prospects for new or additional products and services. The objective of the relationship manager is to use product integration (cross-selling) to protect and increase market share and create win-win situations for the customer and the bank. Thus as bankers develop and manage relationships they can satisfy customer needs while at the same time profitably increase market share.

PROSPECTING

The term "prospecting" was first used during the Gold Rush to describe the search for promising places to find gold. Prospecting is faithful to its original definition of "looking for a place that may be profitably worked." A prospect may be an existing customer who is eligible for complementary or additional products, services, or credit, or a new individual or company with the potential of becoming a customer. Prospecting involves actively searching out and developing new business sources. Prospecting is the action step that follows sales planning; it is the implementation of a sales plan.

Sales planning means setting goals and objectives, developing strategies, and establishing an evaluation system to be used in defining new goals. *Sales* involves prospecting, selling, implementing, and follow-up. The bridge between sales planning and selling is the prospect list. Developing the prospect list is planning, and acting on the prospect list is selling.

Developing a Prospect List

One of the key sales-planning strategies is the development and organization of a viable prospect list. Bankers should identify their market area and determine the types of companies that make up their target market. Once they identify their market, bankers should develop their prospect lists.

Some resources that bankers can use in constructing their prospect lists are:

Bank's own Market Research and Planning Unit (files, records, research).

Present customers (these are usually the best source of new or additional business).

Dormant Accounts (I know you had a relationship with us, and I'd like to find out . . .'').

Customers or suppliers of present customers.

Competitors of customers.

Published materials (such as reports, trade magazines, journals, business pages in newspapers, annual reports, Ayers Directory, Fortune 500 and 1000, Dun & Bradstreet, Moody's, Standard & Poor's, Who's Who).

News clippings.

Chambers of Commerce.

Other professionals (lawyers, accountants).

Referrals from customers (ask present customers with pad and pen in hand).

Colleagues, organizations, professional groups, clubs, personal friends.

Directories in buildings (cold canvas or cold calling).

Telephone directory (commercial).

Smokestacking (driving or walking around and keeping eyes open).

Prospect lists should be updated, deleted, and added to periodically. A Prospect Profile Card should be developed for each entry. Some basic information to include is:

1 Name of company or business.
2 Officers' names and functions.
3 Relationship with the bank.

4   Annual sales volume.

5   Total number of employees and number of employees on site.

6   Zip code (plan calls by zip code to cluster calls).

Developing a prospect list is a part of planning, not selling. The phrase "prospect list" may be misleading because the names appearing on the list are really *"suspects"*; and they become *prospects* after they are rated and approached. Since time is at a premium and some suspects are more viable than others, names appearing on this list should be rated.

Rating Prospects

Bankers should rate their prospects if they want to maximize the hours they spend on prospect calls. The following criteria can be used to assist bankers in rating their prospects and developing their priorities.

1   Prospect is eligible for credit or noncredit business.

2   Identity of decision-maker(s) is known.

3   Prospect's needs are known.

4   Banker has industry expertise.

5   Banker has knowledge of products utilized in the industry.

6   Banker has third-party introduction.

7   Bank has strong reputation in the industry.

8   Bank has strong competitive standing.

9   Bank is preferred to the competition.

10 Prospect's borrowing potential.

11 Time estimate for getting business (days, months, years).

12 Total value of the relationship.

Prospect Ratio

Bankers have to determine the number of prospects they should meet with to achieve their objectives so that they can schedule their sales activities. Unless bankers know their batting average, they will not be able to plan the prospecting activities necessary to meet their sales objectives. Determining the number of prospect calls to be made is an important factor in achieving sales goals and objectives. Certainly the names on the prospect list should far exceed the number of calls to be made. Bankers should determine their own prospect ratio (hit ratio of number or prospects to be contacted to make a sale). Regardless of the factors that influence it (market, competition, etc.), bankers should evaluate their results and strive to develop their own ratio based on the number of calls made to the number of sales made, so they know their ratio.

Factors that bankers can consider in developing their prospect ratios are:

Dollar objective for new business—dollar amount to be achieved over the next year.

Number of new customers needed to achieve objective for new business (determine average value of a customer by dividing total dollar value of all customers by the total number of present customers and then divide that figure into the goal for new business).

Number of prospects to approach to gain an interview (determine the number of prospects that must be approached or called to get an appointment for a sales interview).

Number of sales presentations to produce one new customer (determine from experience approximately how many prospects must be seen to produce one new customer).

Using a modification of this approach, bankers should be able to approximate how many sales calls should be made to achieve their objectives.

Bankers should determine through experience and assessment of results what their sales ratios are and how they compare to other bankers. This is one of the most valuable kinds of information bankers can have, since it enables them to compare and evaluate results and make modifications in scheduling or planning; it also helps bankers set new objectives. This kind of organized prospecting effort results in a sales effort that is more efficient and effective.

Ways to Prospect

Prospecting is the first step in developing new or extended relationships; it involves actively searching out and developing new business sources. A prospect may be an *existing customer* who is eligible for complementary or additional noncredit or credit products or services. A prospect may also be a *new individual or company* with the potential of becoming a customer. Of course it is much more difficult to "prospect" with *new* individuals or companies; therefore prospecting for new relationships will be the primary focus of this chapter. Using their prospect lists or a cold canvass approach, bankers basically have two alternative ways to prospect: the appointment call, or the cold call (a call without an appointment). Regardless of which method they use, follow-up is critical.

Appointment Calls

It is recommended that, whenever possible, bankers arrange appointments in advance. This is particularly appropriate with corporate customers; with small neighborhood businesses or with personal banking customers, it may be more acceptable to make cold calls.

The telephone is the most efficient tool for arranging appointment calls. When calling for an appointment, bankers should, in most circumstances, avoid the temptation to sell over the telephone. Except for Foreign Exchange, Money Desk Transactions, and so on, the telephone should be used to arrange an appointment and no more! The opportunity to meet a customer in person should not be lost by trying the almost impossible (to qualify, interest, explain, probe, sell, and complete the sale) over the telephone. In making the telephone contact with a prospect, the banker's objective should be only to *arrange an appointment*.

Making the Telephone Appointment

To maximize the benefits of the telephone, bankers should appreciate its strengths as well as the limitations. As one of its major strengths, the telephone is an invaluable time saver for arranging to meet with prospects. Bankers should also recognize the limitations of the telephone and limit their conversations to the kind of information included in the opening of their sales calls, in which they *sell the appointment, and not the product.* At all costs, and it will probably cost the appointment, bankers should avoid the trap of trying to sell over the telephone.

Appointment telephone calls with prospects should be limited to:

1 Greeting.
2 Identifying banker and bank.
3 Hinge (mutual point of reference).
4 Possible *value* to customer in seeing banker (based on research or experience or even an educated guess).
5 Request for the initial appointment.
6 Establishing date, time, and place.
7 Confirming date to tie down the appointment.
8 Repeat name ["For your calendar my name is..." (spell it)].

Sometimes, if bankers do not have qualifying information on the customer, they may find it necessary to ask some qualifying questions after stating the possible value.

Telephone Brush-Off Objections

Because of prospects' busy schedules and competitive and business pressures prospects may *resist* scheduling the appointment and offer "brush-off" objections. Typical objections are:

"I'm too busy."
"Send me a proposal."
"My bank provides everything."
"Tell me over the phone what you want, to save time."
"Call _____ , who reports to me."
"We just changed banks."

When prospects pose smoke-screen objections or excuses, they are often really saying, "You haven't convinced me there is an advantage for *me* in seeing you." The customer does not really want a dissertation on the product, but rather wants to know how he or she will benefit from meeting with the banker. In attempting to overcome the objection, bankers *must* guard against selling over the phone and avoid a lengthy product or idea discussion. Since bankers themselves are the most important factor in communicating information, they should not rely on the telephone to establish rapport, credibility, or the time necessary for an effective sales interview.

15-Minute Strategy.   When bankers are faced with brush-off objections, they should use the "15-minute strategy" in which they repeat the objection and restate the possible advantages that may accrue to the prospect through the sales meeting and suggest a 15-minute introductory appointment.

After a prospect refuses to set an appointment, bankers should:

1 Repeat the objection.
2 Restate the possible value to the customer.
3 Go in again for the appointment by requesting a 15-minute appointment.
4 Establish a date and time.
5 Confirm date and time.
6 Repeat name.

The obvious difference between the first request for an appointment and the second request following the customer's objection is the introduction of the *15-minute* time slot. Very often customers will agree to an initial meeting that has tight parameters. Bankers should not lose sight of their main objective, which is to arrange a personal appointment.

The following are examples of using the telephone to sell the interview and not the product after the customer gives a brush-off objection:

Objections	Consultative Telephone Response
I'm not interested.	Mr. _____ , I can understand your not being interested in..., since you have not had a chance to discuss how it may be possible to.... I would

like to meet with you to discuss with you how it may...for your company. I think if we could meet for 15 minutes, you could determine.... Would later this week be convenient or early next week? Tuesday morning at 9:30 or Wednesday at 11:00?

I'm too busy.

Mrs. _____, I can appreciate that you have a busy schedule and that is why I called. I'd like to arrange a 15-minute appointment at your convenience to discuss the way in which...could possibly...so that you could determine if a full appointment.... Would...?

Tell me what your idea is.

Miss _____, ...can be explained clearly and quickly, but by meeting with you for 15 minutes, I could relate it more specifically to your requirements. What time would be convenient for a brief meeting?

Your bank wasn't interested in my business four years ago. You got frightened of my industry and wouldn't talk to me.

I'm sorry to hear that you had the experience with our bank. I'd appreciate the opportunity to meet with you for 15 minutes and discuss the possible ways in which...now. I think you will find the bank has changed and.... Would next week be a convenient time for a meeting?

Send me a proposal.

I will be very happy to send you the information, Mr. _____, but I would like to meet with you for 15 minutes to ensure that the materials are appropriate for your particular situation. Would...?

I can't afford it right now.

Mrs. _____, I can understand your desire to avoid unnecessary expenses; however, it may be to your advantage to review...to determine whether or not it can offset...and possibly reduce.... Would...?

You'll be wasting your time.

I appreciate your consideration; however, it is my feeling that it will take only fifteen minutes to determine the value of...to you. Would...?

I've just changed banks.

I can understand your commitment to a new relationship, but I would appreciate the opportunity to meet with you for 15 minutes so that you can determine the extent to which we may be able to complement your present banking relationship....

My present bank provides everything.	I can appreciate that you have a banking relationship that is satisfying your current needs. I'd like to meet with you for 15 minutes, to discuss...so that you can determine (compare) the possible advantages to you and the way we could possibly complement your present relationship. When later this week?
You'll have to call _____, my assistant.	I would appreciate the opportunity to meet with _____. I will contact him and keep you abreast of the progress. I hope to have the opportunity to meet with you to present...after the initial meeting. (A letter should be sent thanking the customer for arranging or suggesting the meeting and also outlining benefits that *may* accrue to the customer as a result of the meeting. Also if possible bankers should introduce themselves during the call and should send a follow-up letter.)
	If the customer is really the one the banker should see due to distance or corporate input: Mr. _____, I would welcome the opportunity to meet with _____. Since I will be there, I would also like to stop in and introduce myself to you after seeing _____ to.... (This is high and wide selling in which bankers can use the information gathered during the "wide" meeting to sell to "high" personnel.)

These examples are provided to encourage bankers to make a second effort, not of course to be read or used verbatim.

Getting the appointment with a prospect is predicated on the bankers' ability to suggest a *possible* opportunity to the prospect, not on making a sales presentation on the telephone. Each of the blanks in the responses indicates that the bankers did some homework prior to the call. Bankers should work toward setting a brief initital appointment and should use their appointment time to motivate the prospect to extend the time or to set a full appointment. Once bankers succeed in setting the appointment, they should use their fifteen minutes to find out about the prospect's situation, uncover the prospect's needs, and interest the prospect sufficiently in what the bank may be able to do for him or her so that a *full* appointment is set or the present one is extended. When the fifteen minutes are up, bankers should acknowledge it and ask if they should continue, or if a second appointment would be more convenient.

The objections and responses show how bankers can keep sight of their objective to sell a personal sales interview and to retain control of the telephone conversation. Trying to sell on the telephone often results in lost opportunities. "Proposals in the mail" and other nondirect approaches are time consuming and expensive, and their results are often disappointing. Personal first interviews cannot be replaced by phone calls, proposals, or letters.

Telephone Techniques

To help secure appointments with prospects, bankers can also incorporate the following telephone techniques.

Assumptive Opening with Secretaries. When speaking to secretaries, bankers should assume that they will get through to the party they are calling. Rather than asking to speak to Mr. Smith, bankers should say, "Mr. Smith, please.... Tom Brown calling." If Mr. Smith is not available, bankers should jot down the secretary's name and use it during the next call.

Third-Party Referral Openings. Referrals from a satisfied customer, acquaintances, or another third party are invaluable to bankers who are prospecting. "Mr. X suggested I contact you...."

Hinge Openings. Referring to an article in the paper about a new facility, new management or any mutual point of reference that serves to connect bankers with customers are also effective ways to open. "In your annual report..."

Industry Opening. Stating experience with the customer's industry also can motivate a customer to set an appointment. "I have been working with several manufacturing companies..."

New Development Opening. Discussing a new situation or a new product or any change or innovation in the bank or in the company is an excellent way to open. "Our bank has just become a member of X banking group, increasing our ability to provide international services."

General Strategies. Some general telephone strategies for arranging an appointment are:

Send a letter to a difficult-to-reach prospect before the telephone call and use the letter as a hinge in selling the appointment.

Develop rapport with secretaries; ask for and use their names.

Don't try to sell the product—sell the interview.

Use third-party references whenever possible.

Refer to a similar client using your service.

Suggest a new or special aspect of a product.

Suggest a 15-minute or less time frame for a new prospect after a brush-off objection.

Repeat objections before fielding them to show concern for the customer.

Avoid falling into a brush-off trap of sending a proposal without an interview to determine needs.

Meet with someone from the decision-maker's staff if necessary as a first step.

The Cold Call

The second most frequently used method of prospecting is the cold call. A cold call is a personal visit to a prospect *without an appointment.* Experience with bankers indicates that there is confusion concerning the definition of a cold call. Some bankers think it is a call for which they are unprepared, or a first call. Basically, bankers should not waste their time on calls for which they are unprepared. Cold calls as they are used in this book refer to meeting with prospective or established customers without having arranged an appointment in advance.

Cold calls do have a place in certain banking situations. The can never replace appointment calls, but they can *supplement* them. The appointment call may be considered more professional and more polite in certain markets, and they are more effective and time efficient, particularly in the corporate environment.

Why then bother with the cold call? For several key reasons:

1 Cold calls can help bankers maximize prime-time selling by substituting cold calls for canceled or interrupted appointment calls.
2 Cold calls increase the banker's ability to maximize a market area in an out-of-the-way location and ensure the most complete coverage of an area.

3   Cold calls can be perceived positively in some markets as aggressive.

4   Cold calls are an excellent way to fill the time gap between appointment calls, become better acquainted with market areas, and learn about customers and competition.

5   Cold calls provide an opportunity to gather specific information about the company from receptionists, annual reports, personally seeing the facility, and so on.

6   Cold calls provide inexperienced bankers with hands-on experience with customers and the marketplace.

7   Cold calls are a kind of welcome wagon for new small businesses in the area.

8   Colds calls can be used to arrange full appointments.

Limited Objective of the Cold Call.   Although cold calls can be used successfully to round out the banker's schedule and to create a market presence, they are fraught with frustrations and disappointments. The most negative aspects of cold calls are the high rate of rejection and refusal and the possible misuse of time. Cold calls on existing customers are often more accepted or tolerated than cold calling on prospects. Prospects often respond negatively to cold calls because they consider them to be second-rate calls that do not show respect or concern for the prospect or his or her schedule. Nevertheless, cold calls can be valuable *when they are approached with realistic objectives.* When bankers initiate cold calls anticipating immediate results, they are building in their own disappointment, failure, and disillusionment. Although there are some war stories of major accounts being obtained as a result of a cold call, most cold calls are not so instantly productive. *Cold calls should not be used as opportunities to sell a product but rather to uncover needs and sell the idea of the next full appointment. The primary objective for cold calls should be to arrange a full appointment to address the customer's needs.*

Cold calls generally should be used to identify key contacts, gather names, identify possible needs, collect brochures, in-house literature, annual reports, and other such material, and to set a full appointment. If bankers meet with a prospect and something develops because of the bankers' inventiveness, the timeliness of the call, a prospect's immediate need or dissatisfaction with his or her current bank, bankers should take advantage of the opporunity, recognizing that the results exceeded the initial objective. Unless the limited objective of the cold call is understood, cold calling can do more to damage morale than can be offset by the amount of business developed. Like the objective of the telephone prospect call, cold calls should aim at *setting a full appointment.*

Cold Call Objections.   Just as prospects object over the telephone, prospects or their secretaries often resist meeting with bankers during a cold call. As with the telephone call, bankers should not attempt a full sales call when resistance is shown, but rather use the brief meeting with the secretary or the prospect to briefly find facts, gather some names, identify needs, hint at some possible benefits, and *set a full appointment* for another date. If an appointment cannot be set at the time, bankers should leave their cards, send a follow-up letter, telephone the prospect, and use the cold call as the hinge for setting a full appointment.

Persistence and patience are important in making cold calls. Whether it is a receptionist, secretary, assistant, or the prospect himself or herself who puts up a smoke-screen objection to avoid the sales interview, it is the banker's task to earn the customer's attention and time. Making the cold call, leaving business cards, sending follow-up letters, or making follow-up calls all increase the likelihood of getting a full appointment. Cold calls are demanding, but when they are used to *supplement* appointment calls, they can be a challenging and rewarding way to gain experience and increase market share.

Summary

Appointment calls supplemented with cold calls provide an effective approach to prospecting. Follow-through is the heart of all prospecting activities and a simple, workable follow-up system that triggers follow-up calls is critical. In sales, time is money and the time spent in prospecting, identifying prospects, qualifying them, and meeting with them is an investment of sales time that can result in new and expanded relationships.

THE TELEPHONE AS A RELATIONSHIP MANAGEMENT TOOL

Maximizing the Telephone

Telephones are indispensable sales-planning and follow-up tools. They are time savers that should be used to:

Set appointments.

Maintain contact with current customers.

Keep contact with inactive customers.

Reactivate accounts.

Respond to inquiries or problems

Address and sometimes solve customer problems.

Check on progress or decisions.

Gather information.

Follow up on accounts.

Prospect.

Improve internal communications with operations or specialists.

Solve internal and external emergency or long distance problems.

Check names and correct titles, addresses, and so on.

Selling is noticeably absent from this list. Telephone conversations usually cannot replace the personal face-to-face contact that selling requires. With the exception of particular products such as money-desk products, and particular presold customers, telephones should not be used for selling. The primary role of the telephone in *sales* is as a *relationship management tool* for prospecting, arranging appointments, and conducting some preliminary fact-finding, qualifying customers, and following up to check on progress, status, and similar matters.

Planning, research, and homework should precede all telephone calls. Preparation is important if the time, effort, and potential of telephoning are to be realized. Bankers should be prepared with names, titles, dates, and *data.* They should call from a relatively quiet and uninterrupted place and make notes about the specifics of the conversation. Unless there are absolutely no alternatives, phone booths should be avoided in setting appointments or calling customers, since note-taking space and necessary information are often unavailable. Also bankers should flip through their rolodex and tickler file each month to make sure they are maximizing present opportunities and following up as promised or required. The telephone can be a powerful sales-planning and follow-up tool. It can set the stage, monitor progress, and nurture the relationship.

Telephones are time savers when used to prospect, set appointments, and follow up on sales calls. Experience shows that *as instruments for direct sales for bankers, telephones are not effective.* Nor are they very effective in solving serious relationship problems. Nothing can replace the personal visit. The telephone wire can be used to set up and follow up the interview—not take its place. *Used properly, the telephone wire can be the life line of the sale—starting it, holding it together, and holding on to it.* (See pages 136–138 for handling telephone objections.)

NURTURING THE ACCOUNT

The account relationship begins *after* an agreement has been reached and the contract has been signed. Relationships must be cultivated and nurtured if they are to survive. The objective of nurturing is to maintain and expand relationships and to establish long-term relationships that are mutually beneficial to the customer and the bank. Nurturing is an important part of relationship management, since it is the vehicle for follow-up, cross-selling, problem solving, and overall account maintenance.

Follow-up

Follow-up is a mechanism for ensuring customer satisfaction and therefore is essential to relationship management. As relationship managers, bankers should function as a liaison between the customer and the bank to facilitate a smooth start for a new product or service and to monitor the activities of their accounts. If problems arise bankers should play a role in solving them to provide customers with the service and personal attention they require. *Consistent, effective follow-up procedures are perhaps the weakest link in all businesses.* Bankers who provide their customers with efficent and timely follow-up and follow-through are almost always gauranteed of creating their own competititve edge over a large segment of their competitors. To facilitate follow-up, bankers should update their records and complete call reports immediately after the call, initiate appropriate internal actions on a timely basis, and record monitoring and follow-up activities in their own calendars to trigger future activities. Follow-up actions can include providing information to the customer, setting an appointment with a specialist, or installing a product. If there is no specific follow-up, bankers should put a notation in a tickler file and initiate the next personal or telephone nurturing call within a reasonable time span. Energies, progress, and opportunities can be wasted unless there is disciplined follow-up. Follow-up is as important to sales as sales planning, the making of sales calls, or completing sales, and it separates a professional from everyone else.

Cross-Selling

Cross-selling is a valuable by-product of nurturing, since nurturing provides a way to recognize and maximize cross-selling opportunities. The term "cross-selling" refers to providing additional bank products and services to current customers.

All customers who have an account with the bank are targets for cross-selling. Nurturing provides an excellent way to expand the customer base, since present customers are the best sources of additional business. Customers who have a relationship with the bank may frequently benefit from products that complement their present systems or from new products that can meet their other financial and banking needs. For example, a customer who uses several of the bank's cash management products might be a good candidate for computerized balance reporting service. This customer may also be a candidate for other corporate products such as Import Letter of Credit and Foreign Exchange. He or she also may be an excellent candidate for investment instruments such as Certificates of Deposit or Commercial Paper.

Cross-selling is a key factor in developing and keeping market share. Research has demonstrated that the *bond* between customers and the bank is strengthened significantly with each additional credit and noncredit product.

Cross-selling on a consistent basis is not a matter of luck or simply being at the right place at the right time. Bankers must create their own luck by broadening their range of product knowledge and fine tuning their communication skills so that they can recognize and maximize the opportunities that exist with each of their customers. They should apply their product knowledge, customer knowledge, and consultative selling techniques to satisfy all of their customers' needs. To help bankers in their cross-selling efforts, banks often provide computerized systems that give instant access to extensive information on present customers, from which many cross-selling opportunities can be determined. Pertinent information can be used to identify the customer's present relationship with the bank and to project cross-selling opportunities. If bankers do not have computerized resources, they should utilize whatever records are available.

To maximize cross-selling opportunities, bankers should understand how products complement one another and which products are utilized in particular industries. For example:

Customer	Industry	Current Products	Possible Cross-Selling Opportunities
X Company	Importer and exporter of softwear	Letter of Credit (Import, Export)	Foreign Currency Trading (Foreign Exchange) Bankers Acceptance Foreign Exchange Advisory International Cash Management

Cross-selling as a function of nurturing solidifies long-term relationships. It is the vehicle for not only expanding market share but also keeping it. It helps bankers maintain their customer base and reduces loss from attrition. In today's banking environment, banks are aggressively seeking one another's market share. The gentlemen's agreement of the past is not a part of the banking climate of the '80s. Today's bankers must earn their customers' *loyalty* by *building a total banking relationship*, and they must help build in loyalty by satisfying needs through the cross-selling of credit and noncredit services.

Nurturing Calls

Nurturing calls are calls on present customers; they are user calls and should be used to follow-up, keep contact, and cross sell. Nurturing calls are vital, since they protect present relationships from infringements by the competition. They are the *best* way to get additional business, because present customers are the best prospects.

Nurturing calls must be more than "what's new" or "hello" calls. Too often bankers go unprepared for a nurturing call. The objective of the nurturing should be to identify an opportunity to solidify or expand business. Nurturing calls that do not result in the surfacing of problems are apt to be devoid of opportunities. *Bankers should look for problems,* be they bank-related or company-related. Bankers who can help solve problems can strengthen and expand the business relationship. As problems are understood and addressed, bankers can make recommendations that satisfy customer needs, while at the same time promote the products or services of the bank and profitably increase market share.

Nurturing calls require specific preparation. Bankers should refer to sales call reports, files, and records from their last call; analyze and evaluate the status of the account.

Bankers must complete call reports, not just to "push paper" but to document the information that was gathered from the time that was invested with the customer. Memories should never be counted on for recall at a later time. Far too much valuable information is lost when entrusted to memories. Call reports can give bankers or their colleagues instant and complete recall when they are completed and filed properly.

As they open their nurturing call bankers should:

Summarize status to date.

Inquire about customer satisfaction.

State general objective.

Be prepared to look at the overview.

Seek customer comments on conditions or status by asking questions pertaining to the account or industry.

Look for problems.

If a problem arises: discuss problems, ask questions, provide data.

Meet with support personnel if necessary.

Plan next step or corrective step.

Be sensitive for opportunities to cross-sell.

Actively explore cross-selling opportunities.

Utilize the ten elements of a sales call.

Establish and reaffirm the next step or date of next contact.

Summary

Nurturing is a part of sales planning, sales implementation, and sales maintenance. It is the sign of a healthy customer relationship. When nurturing the account, bankers reinforce the confidence that customers exhibited in choosing them and their bank in the first place. Nurturing strengthens established relationships and converts new accounts into a long-term relationship. Nurturing of accounts must take place if attrition is to be reduced and market share is to be increased. Bankers who nurture their accounts are less likely to lose them, and that of course is the basis for expanding market share and building long term relationships.

5

Sales Tips

The sales tips that are listed in Exhibit 4 concern some of the most common difficulties that both new and seasoned bankers encounter during sales calls. These sales tips are based on observation, feedback, and critique of more than one thousand bankers in role-play situations as well as in actual sales situations.

Exhibit 4   Sales Tips

Areas of Possible Difficulty	Situations Before	Analysis	Improvement
Introductions on first prospect calls	**Banker:** I'm Tom Smith.	On first calls it is appropriate for bankers to give some information about their positions at the bank and some information on the bank (three or four minutes is usually sufficient unless the customer expresses a desire for more information) and also to present cards (place cards conveniently for easy access)	**Banker:** I'm Tom Smith, National Division, X Bank (presentation of card). We . . .
Suggesting a possible benefit rather than exaggerating	**Banker:** We definitely have. . . . or We have a fantastic. . . .	It is better to low key the benefits with "may" or "possibly" when first introducing an idea to a customer. Exaggerated claims can damage credibility.	**Banker:** . . . to discuss the ways in which we *possibly* can. . . . or . . . our new service *may provide*. . . .

150

Exhibit 4   Sales Tips (continued)

Not understanding the customer's present situation before selling	**Banker:** We can improve your cash flow by..."	Before discussing a product, bankers should use probing questions to learn about their customers' or prospects' present situation and to uncover needs. Bankers should diagnose before they prescribe. They should test the assumptions they made prior to meeting with the customer, and identify and verify needs before initiating a discussion of a product or offering solutions to problems.	**Banker:** Can you tell me how you are now collecting your remittances? "By utilizing our Lock Box....
Scotchtaping questions	**Banker:** How are you paying for your imports; from what countries do you import; and how satisfied are you with your suppliers?	It is better to ask *one* question at a time, rather than hook a series of questions together. A string of questions is confusing, and questions are apt to get lost. Questions can be specific or general, but they should be asked one at a time.	**Banker:** How are you paying for your imports? **or** Can you tell me a little about your importing operation?

Exhibit 4   Sales Tips (continued)

Giving the customer the opportunity to answer questions	**Banker:** What problems are you having? Are there delays, errors? What we have found is....	Bankers should refrain from answering their own questions, suggesting possible answers, or going into a long explanatory statement. By waiting patiently, bankers can give their customers an opportunity to respond. Although four or five seconds may seem like an eternity, they should learn to wait and be silent if they are to understand their customer's situation or point of view.	**Banker:** What problems are you having?
Listening vs. contradicting the customer	**Customer:** We certainly don't want to speculate. **Banker:** You can't call this speculating.	Rather than contradict the customer, it is preferable to be positive and build on what the customer says.	**Customer:** We certainly don't want to speculate. **Banker:** From what you have said I can understand that speculation is the last thing.... We can help you eliminate the risk....
Using competitive information	**Banker:** Y Bank is known for its impersonal and poor service.	Direct attacks on other banks are unprofessional. It is better to bring	**Banker:** What has been your experience with Y Bank? How

152

Exhibit 4   Sales Tips (continued)

		out their weaknesses by questions or by making objective comparisons about specific features and benefits.	promptly do they (or can they) respond to your inquiries? We provide....
Gathering competitive information	**Customer:** We use two New York banks. **Banker:** We think we can provide....	Bankers should find out who the competitors are, *what is included in the offer, and the price*, to compare price and value.	**Customer:** We use two New York banks. **Banker:** May I ask whom you are using? How have you found...? We can provide....
Knowing competitive information	**Customer:** We use X Bank for our wire transfers. **Banker:** We can provide....	Bankers who are familiar with their competitors' products can be in a position to ask questions that strike at the competitor's weaknesses. By knowing their own product's capabilities as well as their competitors', bankers can highlight their competitive edge.	**Customer:** We use X Bank for our wire transfers. **Banker:** To what extent do you find that there are delays? or How long...?

Exhibit 4   Sales Tips (continued)

Fielding objections	**Customer:** There are too many errors.... **Banker:** Not in our system....	It is preferable to get specifics before trying to resolve objections and to use the Objection Response Model (repeat, clarify, discuss, check for understanding and agreement) as a way to ekep communications open.	**Customer:** There are too many errors. **Banker:** That is a concern, but what specific kinds of errors are you referring to?
Unearthing possible objections	**Customer:** It sounds fine. **Banker:** Great, I think the Zero Balance Account could....	Bankers should raise a major objection that experience indicates will crop up later, when a customer does not raise it. If there are in fact unexpressed possible concerns or problems, bankers can address them and reinforce the benefits in the customer's mind.	**Customer:** It sounds fine. **Banker:** Great. Let me ask you, how do you think your unit managers will react?
Action step with specific closing arrangements	**Banker:** I'll call you in a week or so.	Initiating and implementing the next step is the re-	**Banker:** When next week would it be convenient

Exhibit 4   Sales Tips (continued)

		sponsibility of the banker. A specific time and date should be set at the conclusion of the meeting to facilitate sales actions and reduce the number of "hello calls."	for us to...? 10:30 Tuesday?
	Customer: I'll get back to you in a few days. **or**		That sounds fine. If I don't hear from you by Friday, would it be all right if I contact you to arrange to meet...?
High and wide opportunities—selling to the economic decision-maker (high), and the operations or user decision-maker (wide)	**Customer:** Let me discuss this with the assistant treasurer. **Banker:** Fine, I'll get back to you.	If a customer refers to a third party who will influence or make the decision, the banker should try to meet with the new contact.	**Customer:** Let me discuss this with the assistant treasurer. **Banker:** That sounds like a good idea. What are your thoughts on my meeting with him (or the two of you) to review...?
Joint calls	**Banker:** I'll have our cash management specialist call you to arrange an appointment.	Bankers, whenever possible, should accompany the specialists, since the primary relationship is with the banker. The banker should arrange the appointment rather than	**Banker:** I'll arrange an appointment for our cash management specialists to meet with us.... When next week...?

155

Exhibit 4   Sales Tips (continued)

		leave it to the specialist or the customer to initiate contact.	
Taking notes	Banker automatically begins to take notes.	It is usually advisable to seek a customer's approval before taking notes.	**Banker:** I'd like to jot down some notes if you don't mind, **or** Do you mind if I take these details down?
Criticizing the bank or colleagues	**Banker:** Those operations people down there.... **or** I thought they should have accepted the deal....	Bankers should avoid blaming operations, a credit committee, specialists, or management, as a way to defend or explain a problem or a decision. It will reflect negatively on the bank and the banker eventually. It may seem to be an easy out, but bankers may have to pay for it later.	**Banker:** I'm sorry to hear about the problem. Let me check with our operations people.... **or** We found....
Customer sophistication	**Banker:** Let me explain....	Bankers should not make assumptions about customer's knowledge of a product but rather should inquire how familiar he or she is to avoid being *under* or *over* his or her level. Bankers should take into consi-	**Banker:** How familiar are you with...? **or** What experience have you had with...?

Exhibit 4   Sales Tips (continued)

		deration the position and experiences of the customer.	
Start-up time	**Banker:** We can get you started in a week or two.	Bankers should be *realistic* and *cooperate with operations*, but should not unnecessarily extend start-up time, or it can cost the deal. They should take special situations into consideration. Product start-up time must be competitive and efficient.	**Banker:** When would you need the Letter of Credit? **Customer:** I think we would...in four days.
Bankerese	DTC, LC's, ZBA's, ACH, make a market, basis points, and so on.	Bankers should avoid using jargon when discussing a product to avoid confusing customers.	Depository Transfer Check, Letter of Credit, Zero Balance Account, Automated Clearing House, and so on.
Benefits to the customer	**Banker:** We want to protect your margins, since we have a credit outstanding to you....	Bankers should avoid discussing *benefits to the bank* with a customer. It is preferable to address the product or service as it benefits the *customer*.	**Banker:** We may be able to accelerate the collection of receivables and help reduce your borrowings....

POSSIBLE DIFFICULTIES

Some additional problems that may warrant discussion include:

Voice Over

When the banker and the customer both begin to talk at the same time during the sales interview, the customer *always* has the right of way. Bankers should stop talking and listen.

Nail Down One Product at a Time

Bankers should complete the action step arrangements for one product before addressing a cross-selling possibility, unless it is a package deal. Nail one sale down at a time, or all opportunities could be lost. For example: customer is about to sign up for Certificate of Deposit for his or her company; the banker begins to discuss personal investments, which results in distracting and confusing the first almost-made decision.

Seating Arrangements

During a sales call, bankers should select seating that creates an advocate rather than an adversary position when they are given a choice. Right angles, for selling purposes, are always preferable to head-on (directly across from one another) positions.

Range of Products

Bankers should not approach a call prepared to talk to a customer about only one product, unless they have a direct lead. They should be prepared to uncover needs and apply their *range* of product knowledge accordingly. By doing homework, assumptions can be made about product opportunities, but products should be discussed only after needs are identified.

Desk Space

Bankers should avoid putting their paper, coffee, or other items on the customers desk unless invited to do so. If there is no other option, the banker should ask the customer's permission.

Handouts

Bankers should distribute handouts as they intend to use them, or they may find themselves in competition with the handouts.

Self-Confidence

Confidence is the first and final sales tip. Confidence comes from successes in the field, and success is the result of *preparation* and *practice*. Bankers should do their homework, initiate sales calls, and evaluate their calls and their sales results on an ongoing basis as a way to increase their confidence and effectiveness.

6
Self-Training
in the Field

The objective of this book is to accelerate the development of effective sales skills. Sales training can be addressed in a book, but the integration of the concepts into everyday selling practices must take place *in the field*. Although nothing can substitute for experience, the practical and concrete approach to consultative sales presented in this book has been and can be transferred and applied to day-to-day selling situations.

In the final analysis it is the actual day-to-day contact with the customer that determines sales results. Since bankers are frequently on their own when they are making sales calls, it is important that they analyze their sales call activities as a way to measure and improve their sales effectiveness. For self-training to work, it should be done in a consistent, objective, and organized way. Bankers should not rely on their general feelings about a call to evaluate it. Their self-critique can be most helpful when it is based on specific guidelines, and when an objective set of criteria is used. As a way to assist bankers in applying and integrating the ten elements of a sale into their everyday sales activities, a *Self-Development Checklist* has been developed to be used by bankers after each sales call. By using the checklist presented in Exhibit 5 on a daily basis, bankers can evaluate their sales calls, analyze their results, and when necessary modify their selling strategies.

Exhibit 5   Post Sales Call Self-Development Checklist

	Yes	No
Homework		
Did the customer qualify as a prospect?	_____	_____
Was the contact with a decision-maker or a decision-influencer?	_____	_____
Opening		
Was the proper tone set?	_____	_____
Was the *interview* sold before the product discussion began?	_____	_____
Motivation Lever		
Was the customer's present situation discussed?	_____	_____
Were the customer's needs identified?	_____	_____
Were they satisfied?	_____	_____

Exhibit 5   Post Sales Call Self-Development Checklist (continued)

	Yes	No
Features and Benefits		
Did the product information relate to customer needs?	_____	_____
Was the product knowledge adequate?	_____	_____
Were features linked with customer benefits?	_____	_____
Probing Questions and Incremental Close		
Were probing questions used effectively?	_____	_____
Were incremental closings utilized to test for agreement and understanding?	_____	_____
Did the banker listen constructively?	_____	_____
Was a dialogue developed?		
Objections		
Was the objection response model utilized (repeat, clarify, state features and benefits of product, close incrementally)?	_____	_____
Were objections turned into selling points?	_____	_____
Competition		
Was competitive information adequate?	_____	_____
Were competitors identified?	_____	_____
Was competitive information gathered?	_____	_____
Were alternatives compared for price and value?	_____	_____
Total Offer and Pricing		
Was the total relationship taken into consideration?	_____	_____
Was price related to value?	_____	_____
High and Wide		
Were all participants identified prior to the sales call?	_____	_____
Was there anyone else who should have been included in the meeting?	_____	_____
Should someone else be contacted or met with before the next meeting?	_____	_____
Action Step		
Were definite next-step arrangements made?	_____	_____
Were all participants for the next step identified?	_____	_____

Exhibit 5   Post Sales Call Self-Development Checklist (continued)

	Yes	No
Nonverbal and Sales Environment		
Were the nonverbal signals positive?	_____	_____
Was the seating arrangement observed and maximized?	_____	_____
Control		
Did the banker have control of the sales call?	_____	_____
	_____	_____
Result		
Was the sales objective accomplished?	_____	_____

Index

Reader's
Feedback Summary

Based on your sales and banking experience, please complete the following information.

Overall evaluation of the approach to sales in banking presented in this book:

Evaluation of ten elements of a sale:

Areas of the book to be modified or expanded:

Previous experience with sales and product knowledge training in banking:

Additional comments:

Reader's profile
  Position _____
  Years in banking _____
  Bank or company _____
  Division _____
  Name _____ (Optional)

Kindly return to   John Wiley & Sons, Inc. Publishers
                   605 Third Avenue
                   New York, NY 10158

                   Attention: Linda Richardson
                   c/o Stephen Kippur